SAINTS A

A Brief History of
the Christian Church

by

John Coutts

Salvation Books
The Salvation Army International Headquarters
London, United Kingdom

First published 2007

Copyright © 2007
The General of The Salvation Army

ISBN 978-0-85412-765-8

Cover design by Nathan Sigauke

Published by Salvation Books
The Salvation Army International Headquarters
101 Queen Victoria Street, London EC4V 4EH, United Kingdom

Printed by UK Territory Print & Design Unit

Contents

Foreword

THIS latest volume from the pen of Dr John Coutts is to be warmly welcomed. With characteristic clarity and an instinct for what is important he sweeps us across the centuries of Church history in breathtaking manner.

Naturally, much has been left out since this is intentionally a short volume, written with non-specialists in mind as an introductory overview and an appetite-whetter. It will be especially useful to readers whose first language is not English.

Dr Coutts places The Salvation Army in its historical setting, but sees infinitely more than his own denominational perspective. He writes as a passionate believer, but with scholarly objectivity and an eye for the occasionally absurd.

In welcoming and endorsing this book I pray that it will be used to the glory of God and that readers will be inspired to go deeper still in searching for the hand of God upon his Church both in the past and today.

Shaw Clifton
General
London, July 2007

Introduction

THIS book celebrates 2,000 years of Christian faith and hope. It tells the story of the Church in every continent and across many centuries. Some saints – such as Peter and Paul – are famous. Schools, cities and cathedrals are named after them. Others are known only through worn writing found on broken tombstones. Most are lost to human memory and unmentioned in history books, but known to God. This book tells the lives of outstanding Christians who have tried to apply the teaching of Jesus to the needs of their own day. Their stories provide a brief history of the Church in outline.

There is space to include only a few of the 'great cloud of witnesses' – and because this book is written, first of all, for readers with connections to, or an interest in, The Salvation Army, we show where some of the Army's traditions came from and how the Army's principles fit in with those of the larger Church. This has meant giving extra space to Protestant and Evangelical Christianity in chapters 9 and 10.

Parts of the Christian story are nothing to be proud of. Sometimes faith, hope and charity have been pushed out by pride, greed and intolerance. But through it all, the loving flame of the Holy Spirit has continued to burn.

ONE

YOU SHALL BE MY WITNESS

The Roman Empire

BY the time of the birth of Jesus, the Romans had conquered all the lands around the Mediterranean Sea. After long and bitter civil wars, Augustus Caesar emerged as sole ruler. For much of the first century AD the Roman world was at peace. Latin was the official language of the western part, and Greek of the east.

The sea had been cleared of pirates. Well-made roads connected the cities and provinces of the empire. These allowed the Roman army to move quickly and also helped speed the missionary travels of Paul. Roman money could be spent anywhere from Spain to Jerusalem and every coin carried a stamp with the emperor's head and a political message: 'Disobey me at your peril!'

To keep control of their vast empire the Romans allowed limited freedom to conquered peoples. Local tribes were allowed to worship their own gods. Some cities were granted self-government, and in a number of provinces – such as Galilee – native 'princes' were allowed to rule with the emperor's permission.

Sometimes the Romans identified a local god with one of their own. They decided, for example, that their god of war – Mars – must be the same as the Germanic war god, Tiw. That is why, to this day, Tuesday (Tiw's day in English) is called *Mardi* (the day of Mars) in French.

The Romans meet the Jews

In 63 BC the conquering Romans captured Jerusalem and entered the Temple. This brought them face to face with the Jews, who claimed that their God was supreme and could never be identified with any other. Jewish faith was, and is, based on the Ten Commandments and the Law given by God to Moses. Many Jews also hoped that God would soon send them a deliverer – the Messiah – to establish his Kingdom throughout the world.

The Romans were baffled but allowed the Jews to practise their faith, recognising it as a 'legal religion'. Indeed, some Roman soldiers – like the centurion Cornelius of whom we read in chapter 10 of the Acts of the Apostles – were attracted to the Jewish belief in one supreme God. So when the Christians came along – at first a tiny group – some Romans probably thought they were another strange branch of the Jewish faith.

If so they were wrong, for the Christian Church was indeed something new. Its cradle was the Jewish faith, but it is made up of people who believe Jesus of Nazareth is God's Son, the Messiah, and Saviour of the world. They accept him as their Lord and try, with the help of the Holy Spirit, to live in obedience to his teaching.

Jesus of Nazareth
Jesus grew up in Galilee, a province of Palestine ruled by Governor Herod Antipas. He preached good news – announcing the coming of the Kingdom of God, healing the sick and making friends with outcasts. This led to opposition from leaders of his own people. After a trial before Pontius Pilate, the Roman governor in Jerusalem, Jesus suffered death by being nailed to a cross – the cruel and degrading punishment reserved for traitors and major criminals.

It looked like the end for Jesus and his teachings, but after his shameful death the followers of Jesus began to claim he had risen from the dead. He was the Messiah – the Deliverer promised by God! They stated their faith in simple terms, with joyful affirmation: 'Jesus is Lord' (1 Corinthians 12:3 all quotations from *New International Version*).

Some years later the Jewish writer Josephus recorded brief notes about Jesus and his community. He said, 'The race of Christians named after him is not yet extinct.' How right he was!

2

Making history

Most of the first believers did not take detailed notes of what was happening. They were interested in making history, not in recording it. One exception, and our guide to the early days, is Luke, who wrote the third Gospel and added a second volume, the Acts of the Apostles. Luke was an educated Greek-speaking historian who wrote his work (often called 'Luke - Acts' for short) partly in order to convince Roman readers that the Christian movement was loyal and honest.

We can compare the story told in Acts with information gained from the New Testament letters written by Paul and others. From these we learn that new Christian communities were founded in many major cities of the eastern Roman Empire – such as Corinth and Philippi – as well as in Rome itself. By 56 AD, writing to believers in Rome, Paul was able to say: 'From Jerusalem all the way around to Illyricum I have fully proclaimed the gospel of Christ … I will go to Spain and visit you on the way' (Romans 15:19, 28).

The birthday of the Church

Luke begins his story in Acts by recording the words Jesus spoke to his disciples before he ascended into Heaven: 'You will receive power when the Holy Spirit comes on you, and you will be my witnesses in Jerusalem, and in all Judaea and Samaria, and to the ends of the earth' (Acts 1:8).

The promise was fulfilled on the Day of Pentecost – one of the great Jewish festivals – when a group of discouraged believers met in an upper room in Jerusalem. They had been shaken by the cruel killing of their teacher and leader, although some were claiming he had been raised from the dead by the power of God. That seemed hard to believe until, suddenly, 'A sound like the blowing of a violent wind came from heaven and filled the whole house where they were sitting. They saw what seemed to be tongues of fire that separated and came to rest on each of them. All of them were filled with the Holy Spirit' (Acts 2:2-4). The Day of Pentecost was the birthday of the Church.

3

The Acts of the Apostles paints a vivid picture of the life of the earliest believers. Beginning in Jerusalem, the story ends in Rome – which Luke and his readers regarded as the centre of the civilised world.

The growing Church

Luke shows us that the first believers were united in love, and keen to spread the good news. But he does not hide the problems they faced. Some of these have puzzled the Church ever since.

Which language?

All the first believers were Jews, but the Greek-speaking Jews could not agree with the Aramaic-speaking group about the funds set aside to support the community's widows (Acts 6:1).

Social workers or evangelists?

This disagreement led to the establishment of the first Social Work Department – the so-called 'Seven Deacons' – who were to work alongside the 12 apostles (Acts 6:5). But Stephen, one of the seven, did not confine himself to caring for widows. He engaged in fiery preaching and was stoned to death (Acts 6:8–8:1). A young man named Saul of Tarsus was present at the killing and approved of it. Little did he know as he watched the death of the first Christian martyr that he, too, would one day surrender his life for the faith.

A gospel for all?

At first the good news was shared with Jews only, but then some believers, visiting the great city of Antioch, took the decisive step of preaching to non-Jews. Like many heroes and heroines of the faith, their names have been forgotten. The historian Luke is able to tell us only that 'Some ... men of Cyprus and Cyrene ... went to Antioch, and began to speak to Greeks also' (Acts 11:20).

This raised a difficult question: on what terms should non-Jews be accepted into the faith? Should they promise to keep the entire Jewish law? Should male converts undergo the rite of circumcision? The first believers were deeply divided on the question.

James, Peter and Paul

James the brother of Jesus was the leader of the Jewish Christians, based in Jerusalem. Many of his people were unhappy at the idea of accepting Gentiles. Surely, they thought, if Gentiles accepted Jesus as Lord they should also accept – and keep – the entire Law of Moses. This meant that male converts ought to be circumcised.

By contrast, **Paul** stood for Christian freedom. He argued that salvation came through faith and if you compelled new converts to observe the entire Jewish Law – which he observed himself – then you would make salvation a matter of merit. In his letter to the Galatians he argued strongly against the need for circumcision and criticised James and Peter – the 'so-called pillars' of the Church (see Galatians 2:9).

Peter found himself the man in the middle. He had played a key role at the Day of Pentecost and his missionary travels are recorded in the early part of Acts. His encounter with the Roman soldier, Cornelius, convinced him not to 'call anything impure that God has made clean' (Acts 11:9).

The Council of Jerusalem

How could the disagreement be resolved? At the **Council of Jerusalem**, recorded in Acts 15, an agreement was reached. Peter would be the apostle to the Jews, and Paul to the Gentiles. Circumcision was not essential, and the Gentile Church abroad would give financial aid to the Jewish Church at home in Jerusalem.

A new name: 'Christians'

At first the new faith was simply called 'The Way', but in Antioch – a great multicultural city – the people gave the new believers a new name. Luke tells us, 'The disciples were called Christians first at Antioch' (Acts 11:26).

The word 'Christian' was probably meant as a nickname at first. A follower of Caesar was called a 'Caesarian' so if you followed Christ you must be a 'Christ-ian'. But the nickname soon turned into a badge of honour.

Missionary travels

In writing the story of the Early Church, Luke can only give short examples of how the missionaries worked. He portrays Paul as preaching to a Jewish audience, as well as to the up-country people of Lycaonia, who cannot even speak Greek and mistake him for a god. He also tells the story of Paul's meeting at Athens with the leading Greek philosophers, when the apostle attempts to tell them the truth about 'The Unknown God'.

Paul also tried hard to keep faith with the Jewish Christians in Rome, led by James the brother of Jesus. On one of his visits to the holy city he was arrested. After hearings before two Roman governors – Felix and Festus – he played his last card as a Roman citizen by declaring, 'I appeal to Caesar' (Acts 25:11). The final word is of him in Rome under house arrest, waiting for his appeal to be heard.

But what happened to Peter and Paul?

The author does not tell us what finally happened to Peter and Paul, probably because his first readers already knew. There were many other things about the earliest Church which he takes for granted. We have to read between the lines, for we cannot paint a complete picture of the life of the first Christians.

Where did the believers worship?

In those days there were no church buildings. Christians met wherever they could, often in the larger rooms of wealthier members. At Ephesus, Paul used a lecture hall (Acts 19:9) and at Troas the church assembled in an upper chamber where the atmosphere was so hot and stuffy that a young man named Eutychus fell asleep and fell out of the window (Acts 20:8-12).

How did they worship?

From Paul's letters we learn that worship was spontaneous. Individual members came along with a hymn, a word of instruction or a 'tongue' (1 Corinthians 14:26). But it is possible that the Jewish Christians had a more ordered worship based on the form used in the synagogue.

The Lord's Supper was celebrated as part of a larger fellowship meal at which, apparently, the poor could go hungry (1 Corinthians 11:20-22). Women could prophesy but were expected to cover their heads (1 Corinthians 11:5).

How were they organised?

Over the centuries Christians have studied the New Testament and many have claimed to discover definite plans for 'church order', but they have not agreed as to what they are, and over the centuries their differences have sometimes led to conflict. Disagreements over church order and 'Apostolic succession' divide the various Christian denominations to this day.

Was there ever a single plan for the Church? The New Testament speaks of 'overseers' (bishops), 'elders' (presbyters, a word later shortened to 'priest') and 'servants' (deacons).

The Salvation Army has always taught that no precise plan for the Church can be found in the New Testament because Jesus left his disciples free to adapt their structures to suit local needs.

For the Salvationist, the true 'Apostolic succession' is the succession of the Holy Spirit. General Frederick Coutts (The Salvation Army's international leader from 1963 to 1969) wrote: 'Wherever we find the grace of the Lord Jesus Christ, the love of God and the fellowship of the Holy Spirit, there is the Church.'

Years of crisis: The Great Fire of Rome

The peace established by Augustus Caesar was not to last. In AD 64 much of the city of Rome was burnt down in a great fire. The Emperor Nero, who was losing popularity, looked for someone to blame and chose a very unpopular new sect – the Christians. The

7

Roman writer Tacitus tells us (*Annals* 16:4): 'Punishment was inflicted on the Christians ... they were convicted not so much of the crime of arson but of hatred of the human race ... Punishment of every sort was added to their deaths.'

According to tradition, both Peter and Paul perished in this First Great Persecution, along with many other believers. James the brother of Jesus was dead already. Some Christians might have thought these great troubles would soon be followed by the return of Jesus. If so, they were wrong.

Years of crisis: The Jewish War

In 66 AD the conflict between the Jews and Romans came to a head. A great struggle began, which the Romans called 'The Jewish War'. In the following year Nero was overthrown. In AD 69 there were four Roman emperors in one year. As Roman fought against Roman, Jewish nationalists attempted to drive them out of their lands for ever. For some eager freedom fighters, the 'Kingdom of God' meant an earthly kingdom, with Jews on top and Romans on the run. They thought their day had come at last. They were wrong. The Romans regrouped and in AD 70 Jerusalem was recaptured. The Temple was burned to the ground and the sacred vessels carried away

The Jewish War dealt a cruel blow to Jewish Christianity. The believers fled across the Jordan river, and there the community declined and disappeared.

A time to consolidate

The Church survived the crisis but the great leaders – James, Peter and Paul – were dead. Jesus had not returned. The end was not yet. It was time to consolidate. Evangelists began to collect the stories and sayings of Jesus and to compile the four Gospels, and other gospels which were not to be included in the New Testament. Someone also took the trouble to make a collection of Paul's letters, which were read aloud during worship.

A time to explain

But what was so wrong about Christianity? Why were Christians accursed for their 'hatred of the human race'? To many non-Christians they seemed stand-offish and strange, and there were rumours about their secret meetings. Did they engage in sexual orgies? Or eat babies? In their turn, believers had hard thinking to do – about their own faith and about their relationship with the wider non-Christian world.

A time for clear thinking

The first simple statement of Christian belief declared: 'Jesus is Lord' (1 Corinthians 12:3). But this could mean different things to different people. What *kind* of Lord was he? Some suggested that God had sent a mighty angel or archangel, but the writer of the Letter to the Hebrews protested that Christ is 'much superior to the angels!' (Hebrews 1:4).

Others wondered if the divine Son of God could be truly human. Perhaps he was some kind of phantom? The writer of the First Letter of John declares that only the spirit which 'acknowledges that Jesus Christ has come *in the flesh* is from God' (1 John 4:2). All these and many other challenges of faith and belief would be faced in coming days.

TWO

CHRIST OR CAESAR?

Pliny's problem

PLINY was a successful Roman governor and a good friend of the conquering Emperor Trajan, whose monumental column stands in Rome to this day. As a boy of 15, Pliny had watched the great eruption of the volcano Vesuvius and written a description that is still studied by scientists. But now he faced a different problem – not volcanoes but Christians.

As governor of Bithynia (now part of northern Turkey), round about the year 115 AD, Pliny was concerned because people had stopped attending the temples. Few animals were being offered in sacrifice. This meant that hay was not being sold and farmers were complaining. Far too many people were becoming Christians. So Pliny began a counter attack. He reported his methods to the emperor.

All suspected Christians were brought to court, faced with statues of the Roman gods and of the emperor and commanded to deny their faith by burning incense and cursing Christ. Some, who declared that they had given up Christianity long before, were released. Others admitted to being Christians, but gave up the faith and burnt the incense as demanded. They too were set free. But some Christians refused. Pliny gave them two warnings, then, if they still stood firm, he ordered that they should be put to death as traitors to the Roman state.

Two women leaders tortured

Why were these 'cult members' so obstinate? Pliny wanted to find out. Although he was a 'civilised' governor working for a 'good'

11

emperor, Pliny did not hesitate to order the torture of two slave women who were church leaders.

Pliny discovered that the Christians used to meet early on Sunday mornings and 'sing hymns to Christ as God'. They also made a promise to be honest and to look after each other's property. Formerly they had held meetings in the evening as well, along with a fellowship meal, but these had been discontinued, perhaps in an attempt to avoid the government ban on unregistered clubs.

Pliny's tortures provided no evidence of disgusting behaviour on the women's part. All he had against them was a report of what he called 'an absurd superstition'. So Pliny asked Trajan, was it a crime simply to be a Christian? Was the name itself enough to condemn a person? Or did the accused have to take part in disgusting cult practices, like group sex or eating babies?

In reply the Emperor Trajan told Pliny he had done the right thing. Christians were not to be hunted out, and unsigned accusations were to be ignored. However, when Christians were discovered they must be dealt with firmly. It was an illogical answer. For the next 200 years the growing Church would live with the uncertainty of this threat.

Witnessing for the faith: The Apostolic Fathers
We do not know the names of the Christian women who were tortured. We do not have the words, or the tunes, of the hymns of praise they sang early on Sunday morning. But some other early Christians left writings which have survived. Those who lived and wrote shortly after the New Testament period are known as **The Apostolic Fathers.**

One of them, **Ignatius, Bishop of Antioch,** was arrested and taken to Rome guarded by 10 soldiers. On the long journey he was received with great respect by local Christians and wrote letters to various churches. Seven of these letters have survived. In them, as in the New Testament letters of John, we find warnings against those who denied that the Lord Jesus had been truly human.

12

Ignatius was so eager to die a martyr's death that he wrote to Christians in Rome, telling them not to try to get him a pardon. 'Leave me to be a meal for the beasts,' he wrote, 'for it is they who can provide my way to God. I am his wheat, ground fine by the lions' teeth to be made purest bread for Christ.'

Explaining the faith: The Apologists

Like many believers since, Ignatius seems to have had little interest in the ways of the non-Christian world. But others sought to reach out to unbelievers and show that Christians were neither wicked, treacherous nor crazy. They are known as 'The Apologists' (in Greek the word *apologia* means 'defence' or 'explanation', so an 'apologist' is an 'explainer').

One of them – the otherwise unknown 'Writer to Diognetus' – declared: 'Christians are not distinguished from the rest of mankind by country or language or customs … They share all things as citizens, but suffer all things as foreigners. Every foreign land is their native place and every native place is foreign. They pass their lives on earth, but they are citizens of Heaven … we may say that Christians are to the world what the soul is to the body.'

Justin Martyr

One of the best-known apologists was Justin Martyr, who dedicated his writings to the emperor – though it is unlikely the emperor read them. Justin was born at Neapolis, now Nablus, in Palestine. He had studied many religions and philosophies and had been impressed by the courage of the Christian martyrs before meeting an old man who pointed him to the Christian faith.

Unlike some other converts, Justin did not condemn all his former beliefs. Instead he tried to live as a Christian philosopher, wearing the philosopher's cloak that was the uniform of pagan teachers. He also argued that some of the great Greek thinkers, such as Socrates, had been 'Christians before Christ'.

'Those who lived with reason,' he declared, 'are Christians, even though they were thought atheists.' They had searched for the truth about the Word of God and now that Word had appeared on earth in Christ. The Word which 'gives light to every man' (John 1:9) 'became flesh' in Jesus (John 1:14).

Throughout Christian history there have been many believers who have tried to explain the faith in terms of their own culture. Justin was a pioneer, but in the year 165 AD, after moving to Rome and working as a Christian teacher, he found himself standing before the Prefect Rusticus, who warned him, as Pliny had done: 'Agree together and sacrifice to the gods.' Justin refused. With six of his converts he was scourged and then beheaded. 'Justin the Explainer' was now 'Justin Martyr'.

The perils of success
The Church continued to grow. In the triumphant words of Tertullian, another of The Apologists, 'The more you mow us down, the more we grow.' But rapid growth brought new challenges.

Church buildings appeared. Many copied the design of the public buildings of the Roman Empire. A regular organisation grew up as well, based on the 'threefold ministry' of bishops, priests and deacons. The bishop was now the head of the Church in a local community. He was assisted by priests, who celebrated Holy Communion, and by deacons.

Women were excluded from leadership in the mainstream Church, though they served as prophetesses in the Montanist movement which had some points in common with the Pentecostal churches of today. In some places, especially in the eastern part of the empire, Christianity became fashionable, so that the Church attracted large numbers of nominal members.

A crisis in Church and Empire
By 200 AD the Roman Empire had stopped expanding. The Roman army could no longer expect easy victories over the so-called savage and barbarian tribes. Powerful nations were pressing forward along the empire's long northern frontier.

First and most dangerous were the warlike Goths, who broke through the frontiers in 248 AD. To beat back the Gothic menace the Romans found an old-style fighting emperor – Decius – who wanted to revive the great days of the conquering Trajan. To win an old-style victory you needed the old Roman religion, so, for the first time, Decius ordered that *everyone* in the empire should sacrifice to the gods and obtain a certificate to prove it. Decius did not expect Christians to stop worshipping on Sundays, but he wanted them to put duty to the empire before loyalty to Christ.

It was a disaster for the Church. Nominal Christians surrendered in droves, sometimes led by their own church leaders. Some rushed to sacrifice, burning the forbidden incense. Some tried bribery. Some anxious parents 'bought' certificates to save their Christian children. Others tried to leave town, or simply lay low. A minority – the martyrs – stood firm and were put to death. Others, the 'confessors', went to prison and were ready to die.

But the Emperor Decius did not rule for long. He led his army into a swamp where they were wiped out by the Goths. The next emperor called a halt to the persecution and left the Church to lick its wounds. Far too many Christians had surrendered and their failure led to divisions in the Church, notably between those who took a strict line and those who were willing to allow the 'lost sheep' to return, perhaps too quickly. Similar problems have often arisen when Christianity becomes a popular movement.

The last great persecution

The Decian persecution (AD 250) did not stop the growth of the Church. Who, then, should the Romans blame for the slow decline of the empire? The disloyal Christians who refused to seek the blessing of the old Roman gods, or the non-Christians who refused to accept the new faith and so caused the wrath of the true God to descend upon them? This question lay behind the last great persecution, under the **Emperor Diocletian.**

By the late third century the Church had become a mass movement. Its leaders were often important people in local society.

In the major city of Nicomedia a large church stood not far from the imperial palace.

Once again the Roman state was threatened with collapse under the attacks of the Goths and other 'barbarian' tribes. Was it not plain that the Roman defeats were the fault of those disloyal Christians who refused to do their duty? When sacrifices were offered to the gods, pleading for victory, Christian military officers were seen to turn their backs – and this at a time when the emperor was fighting hard to restore and reorganise the empire.

At first Diocletian looked for a compromise. Christians who refused to take part in pagan religious ceremonies should be excluded from top jobs in the army and the civil service. But his pagan advisers persuaded him to go further. The church at Nicomedia was demolished and the last great persecution began.

Hunting for Bibles

At Cirta, in north Africa, the town's mayor went on a Bible hunt. He sent his officers to collect and destroy all copies of the Scriptures, which at that time were all handwritten. Church leaders did their best to put him off. Four readers handed over their copies, while another said he had none. The last reader was out, but his wife handed over his copy. A silver box and a silver lamp were also 'discovered' behind a barrel. 'You would have been a dead man,' said the mayor's clerk, 'if you hadn't found them.'

Some were to be dead men indeed. Among the martyrs was a soldier called George, who (probably) died at Lydda in Palestine. In later years his story was to grow, much mixed with pagan legend, until he became the famous 'St George' who killed the dragon – the patron saint of both England and Moscow. Thus did the last leaders of pagan Rome try to wipe out the religion that seemed to threaten their empire and way of life. But what if they were wrong? What if the new faith was true after all?

THREE

IN THIS SIGN, CONQUER!

BY 300 AD the Roman army was very different from the one we read about in the New Testament. It included many foreign soldiers who had come to seek their fortune. Among them was Crocus, king of the tribe of the Alemanni, from southern Germany. Crocus and his men were posted to northern Britain and found themselves in the city of Eboracum (now known as York). Here they were serving with an ambitious young general called Constantine. To this day the great Minster (church) of York stands above the ruins of the Roman government headquarters.

A junta of generals had seized power from the ageing Diocletian and the ambitious young Constantine had been left out of the deal. He was not hostile to Christians and thought the Great Persecution was doing nothing to save the empire. Constantine seems to have put his faith not in the old Roman gods but in one all-powerful god – *Sol Invictus*, 'The Unconquered Sun'.

In 311 AD, Crocus and his men, with other soldiers, proclaimed Constantine emperor. This could only mean civil war, another of the Roman-versus-Roman battles which had weakened the empire. With a small but mobile army, the ambitious Constantine set off to challenge the mighty Maxentius who was ruling in Rome as emperor of the west.

Constantine's army left Britain, crossed the sea into Gaul (now France) and marched on over the mountains into Italy. His men set out under the symbol and the protection of the Unconquered Sun, but before the decisive battle Constantine saw a miraculous sign in the clouds – a cross with the message, 'In this sign, conquer!'

He ordered his men to replace the sun emblem on their shields with the sign 'XP' (in Greek, *chi-rho* – KH-R). These Greek letters form the first two letters of the name *Khristos* – 'Christ'.

Few expected Constantine to win, but as the challenger approached the walls of Rome, Maxentius led his men out to battle and was caught at the Milvian Bridge on the outskirts of the city. He and his guards were swept to their deaths, many drowning in the River Tiber.

It came as an amazing surprise to the entire empire, but there was more to come. When the victorious Constantine met the eastern emperor they agreed to share power. The Edict of Milan (AD 313) put a stop to persecution of the Church, the two emperors declaring: 'Our purpose is to grant both to the Christians and to all others full authority to follow whatever worship each man has desired.'

A miracle! Free at last?

To the hard-pressed Christians it seemed like a miracle. The Roman Empire could not beat them so it had joined them! Praise the Lord! Christianity was now the most favoured religion. The Church was conquering the world! Or was the world taking over the Church?

What kind of conversion?

There are three possible explanations of the conversion of Constantine. It could be true, and he really did see a miraculous sign in the clouds. That was the view of Eusebius, the great historian of the Church. But others argue that Constantine was a cynical pretender who adopted the Christian faith for purely political reasons. Christ and *Sol Invictus* were all the same to him. He wanted power. It is certainly true that after he took over the entire Roman Empire, he executed his own son and wife and had barbarian kings thrown into the arena to be eaten by wild beasts. He was only baptised on his deathbed.

The third explanation, and perhaps the most likely, was that Constantine's head was converted but not his heart. He was convinced of the truth of the new religion and wanted to use the Church to unify and strengthen the empire, east and west.

A divided Church: Arius and Athanasius

If so, he was to be disappointed. The all-powerful emperor discovered that Christians were arguing about the very nature of their faith. Some of them came straight out of jail to debate the Trinity. Christians were divided about the nature of God himself. It was said that if you went to get your hair cut, the barber would ask you if God the Father was greater than God the Son.

Their first creed was the simple 'Jesus is Lord'. This had been developed into a statement known as the Old Roman Creed, very similar to the Apostles' Creed which is recited in many churches to this day. But this had not settled the problem: who was Christ, and what was his relationship to God the Father? Was the Word who became flesh part of the very nature of God, or was he a great but separate being, created by God before or at the very beginning of time?

Arius, an Egyptian theologian, took the latter view. He taught that God created the Word (Christ) first of all, and then brought all things into being through him. You could say that the Son was 'unlike' the Father. His supporters had a slogan: 'There was [a time] when he [the Word] was not [in existence].' This may have been good logic but it was bad religion. It was as if God had not intervened to save the world but had sent his secretary instead.

The opposite view was maintained by the followers of **Athanasius,** who declared that God the Word was 'of one substance' with the Father. To settle the question Constantine called a great conference – the Council of Nicaea (315 AD). Free public transport was provided for Church leaders, some of whom had been in jail not long before. No wonder they thought it was providential! The emperor addressed the council in person, and in the end the Church leaders backed the Athanasian view, affirming that God the Son was 'of one substance with the Father'. The Arians were expelled from the Church and some were sent into exile by the state.

But they still had friends and supporters. Many middle-of-the-road Christians thought it would be enough to say that God the Son was 'like' God the Father. This vague word could mean different things to different people.

Christianity in triumph?

In spite of disputes, the Church went on growing in power and influence. In 381 AD the Emperor Theodosius proclaimed Christianity the state religion of the empire, declaring, 'Let the meetings of the heretics cease.' This meant that non-Christian worship was now banned, or at least driven underground. Breakaway and minority churches also came under pressure to conform. The Church – now closely linked with the Roman state – had come a long way since Pentecost.

Constantinople – the 'second Rome'

Power within the Roman Empire had shifted to the east, and the capital of the empire was moved from Rome to Byzantium, which was renamed the new Christian city of 'City of Constantine', or 'Constantinople'. In the eastern churches the great emperor was declared to be *isapostolos* – 'equal to the apostles'. Thus began the Constantinian era of close Church-state cooperation, which was to last for many centuries. But had the gospel won over the world, or was the Church being taken over by the state? In 385 AD a Spanish teacher – Priscillian – became the first Christian 'heretic' to be put to death for false beliefs. Sadly, he was not the last.

The monastic movement

In a worldly Church, often crowded with nominal Christians, sincere believers began to look for new ways to serve God. For example, Antony in Egypt sought solitude in the desert, where he wrestled in prayer with the temptations of Satan. But he soon became a celebrity. The more he tried to get away, the more people followed him.

Thus arose the calling of the 'monk', dedicated to a life of prayer. 'Monk' derives from the Greek *monos*, meaning 'one only', and refers to the original monks living alone. But isolated hermits could be subject to strange delusions and temptations, so soon the solitary souls gathered into communities for prayer and study. For many centuries (continuing today) the monastic movement has played a decisive part in the life of the Church. Many religious societies have been set up for both men and women.

Famous names in the monastic movement include:

Pachomius (290-346)
A former soldier in the Roman army, Pachomius founded a monastery on the banks of the Nile. His holy living and soldierly discipline attracted large numbers of spiritual seekers to join him, so that by the time of his death there were nine monasteries for men and two for women living under his rule. Monastic life is important in the Egyptian (Coptic) Church to this day.

Basil the Great (330-379)
In the Eastern Church the monastic movement was organised by Basil of Caesarea. In Cappadocia (modern Turkey) Basil had played an important part in defining the doctrine of the Trinity (Father, Son and Spirit – Three-in-One). He was also a great organiser, establishing hospitals and hostels for the poor, who were supported by a system of social security. Basil provided a rule for monks, who were to practise self denial as a form of service to God and the community. Regular hours of prayer and community worship were established, and monks were expected to provide education and care for the poor. The Rule of Basil – laid down between 358 and 364 – still forms the basis of the monastic life in the churches of the east.

Benedict of Nursia (c 480-547)
Benedict played a similar role for the churches of the west. His rule provided that monks and lay brothers should live in common,

21

sharing in prayer, worship, study and manual work. Their life was to be disciplined, but not over-strict.

Benedict founded a great monastery at Monte Cassino in central Italy which remains the chief house of the Benedictine order to this day – though the buildings had to be rebuilt after total destruction in a bitter battle during the Second World War.

The religious life practised by monks and nuns has remained a powerful spiritual force in the life of the Church. Monks and nuns make a threefold vow to seek to follow the 'counsels of perfection': chastity (which includes remaining unmarried); poverty (having no personal property); and obedience (to one's spiritual superior). But does the monastic ideal imply a double standard, with first- and second-class Christians? Were not all believers 'called to be saints'? One day these questions would be asked with passion.

Christian endeavour – outside the empire

Among the Goths
Fortunately believers did not spend all their time arguing about the doctrine of the Trinity.

Translating the Bible
Ulfilas (c 311-383) was a young Goth who was taken captive and sold into slavery. He became a Christian and longed to take the good news back to his own people. He became a missionary and decided to translate the Bible into the Gothic language. He began with the Gospels. We are told he left out the Old Testament books of Kings, which record the battles of the ancient Israelites, because he thought the Goths knew quite enough about fighting already! But this story is probably anti-Gothic propaganda.

Ulfilas was a pioneer in the work of Bible translation – so essential for the work of the gospel right up to today. The Gothic language, an ancient form of German, died out, but a beautiful copy of his translation – partly written in silver lettering – is preserved at Uppsala in Sweden. Unfortunately Ulfilas received the faith in its Semi-Arian variety, believing that God the Son was 'like' the Father. This meant the Goths did not accept the Christian faith in its orthodox form.

To the east: Gregory the Illuminator (ca.257-332)
Among the many missionaries who took the good news outside the boundaries of the Roman Empire was Gregory the Illuminator. He worked in the kingdom of Armenia. Here the royal family were converted, and Armenia became the first-ever 'Christian country'. Gregory became the *catholicos* (head of the Church) and for several generations the post remained in his family.

Into Africa: Frumentius (330-380)
The Church was already well established in Egypt. Tradition tells of Frumentius, who was sent by the great Athanasius to travel up the Nile and establish the faith in the kingdom of Aksum. And the 'Nine Saints' from Syria took the faith to Ethiopia. There they founded monasteries and translated the Bible into Ge'ez, an ancient Ethiopian language. Thus the Christian faith was carried far beyond the bounds of Roman civilisation. It was just as well, because the Roman Empire was about to fall apart.

Top: Statue of Augustus Caeser ; (inset) Roman gold coin; **above left:** Justin Martyr (Justin of Caesarea); icon of the martyrdom of Ignatius.

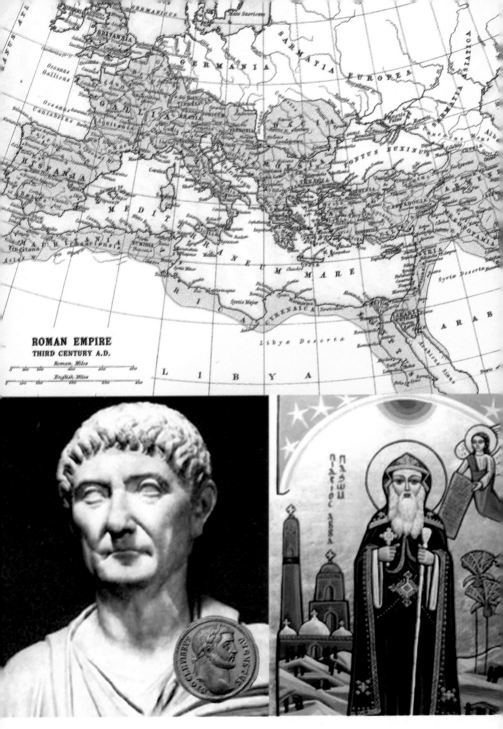

Top: map of the Roman Empire in 200 AD; **above left:** the Roman Emperor Diocletian; (inset) coin depicting Diocletian; (Abba) Pachomius (Pakhom); **opposite page:** map of Byzantine Constantinople.

Map of
BYZANTINE CONSTANTINOPLE.

Drawn by F. R. von Hubner for and under the direction of Professor A. van Millingen.

Scale of 1:30,000

English Miles

Top left: Basil the Great; **right:** Gregory of Tours; **above:** Norse Crusaders offering their services to the Emperor Constantine.

FOUR

THE CITY OF GOD

THE Emperor Theodosius was the last Roman to rule an undivided empire. In the winter of 406/7 AD a great host of 'barbarians' crossed the frozen River Rhine. Much of the Western Empire collapsed, and while the Eastern Empire – based on Constantinople – remained strong, the last puppet emperor in Rome was deposed in 476 AD. What could it mean? Ever since Luke wrote the Acts of the Apostles, Christians had tended to identify their faith with the cause of the Roman Empire. Now it looked like the end of the world they knew. Among the thinkers who wrestled with the problem was Augustine.

Augustine (354-430) was born in Tagaste, in northern Africa. As a young man he lived a dissolute life, with many sexual partners and a regular concubine, who bore him a son, called Adeodatus. But his Christian mother Monica went on praying for him, even when he was running wild.

Augustine made his living as a Professor of Rhetoric, teaching the art of public speaking, which the Greeks and Romans thought very important. As an intellectual with a good knowledge of Latin and Greek, Augustine found the style and stories of the Bible crude, and thought the Church uncultured and ignorant. This led him to join the religion of the Manichees, who dismissed the teaching of the Old Testament. But their faith failed to satisfy Augustine for long.

Augustine moved to Rome, where he spent a long time in personal doubt and confusion. Next he moved to Milan, in northern Italy. Still a popular teacher, he hoped to gain a top government post. But at Milan he came under the influence of the great Bishop Ambrose.

Ambrose (330-397) had been state governor of Milan until he was drafted to serve as bishop and church leader by the popular demand of the Christian population. As Augustine listened to the sermons which Ambrose preached in the cathedral, he heard what seemed to him convincing arguments for the truths of Christianity. As a Professor of Public Speaking, he was also impressed by their beautiful style. Augustine was already reading the works of Greek philosophers, which told him, 'In the beginning was the word, and the word was with God.' But they did not go on to affirm that 'the Word became flesh'.

By now Augustine was strongly attracted to the gospel but still reluctant to live a life of chastity, which for him meant a single life of sexual self control. In the summer of 385 AD he went on retreat with some friends, not far from Milan. While there, in a garden, he heard a child's voice singing 'Take up and read ...' So he took up a copy of Paul's epistles and read: 'not in orgies and drunkenness, not in sexual immorality and debauchery, not in dissension and jealousy' (Romans 13:13). These words led to Augustine's conversion. At Easter 381 he was baptised by Ambrose, along with his son.

Augustine parted from his concubine – whom he did not marry – and went back to North Africa. Here he hoped to live a quiet life of spiritual reflection. But he too – like Ambrose – was forced by popular demand to become first a priest and then a bishop. For good or ill, Augustine's work as a Christian thinker and administrator was to have huge influence on the later history of the Church.

Augustine and Church unity

North African Christianity was divided between the official Church – the 'Catholics', to which Augustine belonged – and the 'Donatists'. The split went back to the Great Persecution, when some Christians had handed over copies of the Scriptures to the state police. Such people were called 'traditors' – our word 'traitor'. The Donatists regarded them as sell-outs who had contaminated the Church. This meant that the Catholics (Augustine's church) had compromised with the traditors, making the Donatist Church the only pure church in existence. The Catholics answered that their church was spread throughout the world, while the Donatists existed in only one province. Like Noah's ark, the Universal Church found room for clean and unclean beasts. A priest might be unworthy – even ordained by a 'traditor' – but God could still work through him.

The Donatist Church could also be seen as a North African nationalist movement, and the government wanted unity. From 405 AD the state began to put pressure on the Donatists to merge with the Catholics. Augustine was reluctant to agree. He knew full well that nobody could be made a Christian by force. But he came to think that 'moderate' persecution (though not the death penalty) might sometimes be justified. Did not the Lord Jesus say: 'Make them come in' (Luke 14:23)? It was a misreading of Scripture which would cost the Church dear in later centuries.

In 412 the emperor banned the Donatist Church, which then went underground. Augustine still felt uneasy but now he had other problems too.

The debate about Original Sin

Christians agreed that men and women were sinners, and that they could not be saved without God's help and mercy. But how and when did they become sinners? Is a newborn baby a sinner? The Church had never defined its position.

Augustine took a pessimistic view. He argued that all mankind sinned in a lump when Adam fell. The taint of original sin was passed on from Adam in the act of sexual intercourse. While Justin Martyr had taught that a righteous pagan like Socrates was a 'Christian before Christ', one of Augustine's supporters taught that the good deeds of the heathen were merely 'splendid vices'. This meant that a baby which died before it was baptised could not be saved, even though it would not suffer pain in the afterlife, and the number of souls saved would eventually equal the number of angels lost when Lucifer rebelled against God and fell from Heaven.

Pelagius

Round about 400 AD a monk named Pelagius arrived in Rome from faraway Britain. He thought Augustine's teaching was far too pessimistic. He taught that Adam's sin does not contaminate the rest of humanity. We ourselves become sinners only when we imitate Adam and choose to do wrong. Original sin is not linked to sexuality, and the married state can be just as holy as the single life. Newborn babies indeed ought to be baptised, but this does not mean they are sinners from birth. The commandment of Jesus to 'Be perfect' is tough, but we can, and should, try hard to live up to it. For this we need God's help, his 'grace'. What is more, the Lord who said 'Be perfect' also said 'Blessed are the poor'. This means it is wrong for the rich to exploit the poor or for the state to use torture.

Augustine was shocked. To him it seemed that Pelagius denied the reality of sin, twisted the meaning of 'grace' and taught self-salvation through personal effort. A huge controversy developed.

Once again the government was worried. In AD 418 the Pelagians were banished from Rome as a threat to peace. They lost the political struggle but while the Church condemned Pelagius's teaching on sin it did not accept all of Augustine's teaching either. Deep questions about God's grace and human free will would come back to perplex believers in later centuries.

The City of God

Throughout the Western Empire, new tribes and nations were on the rampage, and in 410 the unthinkable happened. An army of Goths captured the 'eternal city', Rome itself. Why? To non-Christians the reason was obvious. Many Romans had abandoned the old Roman gods and adopted Christianity, so the gods had given up on them. Christians had claimed that the new faith would revive and renew the Roman Empire. Now look at what had happened!

In reply, Augustine spent many years writing *The City of God*. In this great work he argued that the gospel did not depend on the Roman Empire. The faith would survive its downfall and would have the task of converting the new barbarian masters.

That task Augustine would leave to others. The so-called barbarians did not stop at capturing Rome. The Vandals – a nation related to the Goths – crossed into North Africa to set up a kingdom for themselves. Augustine died in Hippo in 430 while the city was under siege and the Vandal army was seeking to break down its defences.

FIVE

THE DARK AGES

A light in the Dark Ages

THE next 300 years are sometimes called 'The Dark Ages'. If this label seems to suggest that people were more wicked than usual, then it is misleading. The ages are only 'dark' because we do not have much detailed information about them.

New kingdoms were founded on the ruins of the Roman Empire. The gospel was preached all over western Europe. Education was preserved and provided in monasteries. Many wandering missionaries spread the word and later, much later, stories of their lives were told. In Cornwall – the western extremity of Britain – we find villages with names like St Tudy, St Teath, St Petroc and St Enodoc. These were local priests who gave their names to the villages where they worked. Some 'Lives of the Saints' were written but, sadly, most contained more legend than fact.

Patrick, patron saint of Ireland, is an exception. He wrote his own story, and a copy of what he wrote has come down to us. We can compare the real Patrick with the Patrick of legend.

Patrick the slave-boy

When the Western Empire collapsed, Roman Britain was cut off and came under attack from all sides. Raiders crossed the sea from Ireland, wrecking, killing and carrying hundreds away into slavery. One was a young man called Patricius – better known as Patrick.

Patrick's father was a deacon – or maybe a decurion, the spelling is uncertain. A deacon is a church official while a *decurion* was a Roman town councillor. Roman culture had survived in western Britain but there were no legions to defend the people any more. Patrick was only 16 when he was kidnapped and taken across the sea to Ireland. There he was sold to a man who took him to the far west. As a slave, Patrick had to work as a farmhand. Sometimes he tried to explain the gospel, but with little success.

'After I came to Ireland I had to tend sheep every day, and every day I prayed and one night I heard in my sleep a voice saying to me, "Soon you will go to your own country." Then, after a short time, I heard a voice saying to me, "See, your ship is ready."'

It was very dangerous for a slave to run away but Patrick was young and strong. He reached the coast and found a ship, but the captain refused to take him on board. Sadly, Patrick went back to his hut, and began to pray. Then he heard someone shouting, 'Come on, hurry, we shall take you ... make friends with us.'

So Patrick left Ireland and after many mysterious wanderings reached Britain again. Here he was at home among his own 'civilised' people. They begged him to stay.

'But then,' he writes, 'I saw in the night a vision of a man whose name was Victoricus, coming as it were from Ireland with countless letters. The opening words were The Voice of the Irish – and in that moment I heard their voice, "We ask you, holy youth, to come and walk among us once more."'

Was it a true vision? The call was confirmed when a voice said, 'He who laid down his life for you is speaking in you.' Patrick awoke full of joy. To him this could only be the voice of Christ.

So Patrick collected a group of companions and returned to bring the Christian faith to the land which had enslaved him. He had a hard struggle. Churches were founded but now raiders came in the opposite direction, from western Scotland. Patrick's converts were attacked, and newly-baptised women were shared out for the pleasure of their captors. Yet their king – Coroticus – claimed to be a Christian! The fearless Patrick sent him an angry letter. Other nations, he declared, raised money to ransom Christian captives from slave-raiders. 'Far from the love of God,' he declared, 'is a man who hands over Christians to the Picts and Scots.'

Facts and legends

Many stories were told about Patrick and the other saints of that time. It was said Patrick drove the snakes out of Ireland (untrue) and that he used the three-leaved shamrock to explain the mystery of the Trinity to his converts – which is unlikely but could just be true.

The growth of Christendom: Gregory of Tours

The downfall of the empire left a gap in which the Church began to take over some of the role of the state. Ambrose had already exchanged the post of state governor for Church leader. Now, in the power vacuum, bishops began to behave like provincial governors. And why not, if there was no one else to do the job? In some countries, even today, the churches are left to prop up civil society when the state collapses

Among these powerful bishops was Gregory, Bishop of Tours, in Gaul (now France). His cathedral, dedicated to St Martin, was a place of worship, a base for evangelism, a shelter for people possessed by demons, and also a refuge for asylum-seekers. The cathedral was holy ground, so defeated warlords were safe once they got inside, but their enemies would be waiting to kill them once they came out, unless Gregory was able to arrange a truce.

One such fighter-in-hiding was Merovech. Sheltering in the cathedral, he practised 'biblical lots' – picking a Bible text at random to find out what would happen to him. In the prophets he found, 'The Lord will deliver thee into the hands of thine enemies.' And in the Psalms he read, 'You cast them down into destruction.' And when he tried the Gospels he found, 'The Son of Man is betrayed.' Poor Merovech decided he was doomed, and he was right.

Modern Christians might think that this is not the best way to seek guidance from the Scriptures. And while Gregory's faith and courage are examples for ever, we should not follow his medical practice. When he felt ill Gregory made up his own medicine, consisting of water mixed with dust from St Martin's tomb. He believed it made him better.

A new King David?

The kings who struggled for power in Dark Age Europe needed all the help churchmen like Gregory could give. One of them, Constantine, son of Fergus, ruled the Picts and Scots in the eighth century. The name 'Constantine' links him with the first Christian emperor. His people, now Christian, erected a great cross which still stands. A carving on the cross shows the biblical King David, playing his harp. 'Look,' said the king's splendid monument, 'your king succeeds to the glories of Rome, and he also rules like the righteous David in the Bible.'

The rise of the papacy

But in fact there was no longer an emperor in Rome. In the east, the Roman Empire, now based on Constantinople (Byzantium), remained a mighty power, but in western Europe some of the glory of the former Caesars passed to the Church. The title Pontifex Maximus ('Chief Bridge Builder), once borne by the emperor, was taken over by the Bishop of Rome, who is still known as the 'Pontiff'. Throughout the lands of the former Western Empire, kings, churchmen and common people naturally looked to the Church in Rome for guidance, as they might seek help from the United Nations today.

The Emperor Trajan had erected a great monument to record his greatest victories, which still stands in Rome to this day. But the great conqueror who advised Pliny on how to deal with Christians never dreamt that in 1588 AD his image would be removed from the top and replaced by one of St Peter.

A successor to Peter?

Matthew's Gospel (16:18) tells us that Jesus said to his disciple, Simon the fisherman: 'You are Peter, and on this rock I will build my Church.' The name *Petros* (*Cephas* in Aramaic) certainly means 'Rock'. Roman Catholic Christians believe Jesus intended Peter to be the leader of his followers, and that Peter's authority passes on to his successors, the Bishops of Rome. The Pope, therefore, as successor to Peter, is seen by Roman Catholics as the rightful leader of the worldwide Church.

Here is a major difference among Christians, for this claim has never been accepted by the Orthodox churches of the East, and was rejected by Protestants during the Reformation. In the 17th century the English philosopher Thomas Hobbes (1588-1679) declared that the papacy was 'the ghost of the deceased Roman Empire, sitting crowned upon the grave thereof'.

The coming of Islam

A new cloud appeared on the Christian horizon. In 622 Muhammad began the preaching of Islam. After his death, Arab invaders quickly conquered Palestine, and what is now known as Iraq, Iran and Egypt. The holy city of Jerusalem was no longer controlled by Christians. The Eastern Empire was gravely weakened. In 1453 the last Roman Emperor, Constantine XIV, died fighting as Constantinople fell to the Turks.

The new Muslim rulers recognised Christians and Jews as 'People of the Book' – protected minorities, members of tolerated but second-class religions. Christians were encouraged to become Muslims, but Muslims were forbidden to become Christians. In Egypt and the Middle East, the Christian churches slowly declined in numbers, and in North Africa they disappeared completely. The Arab and Islamic advance continued through North Africa and into Spain, but failed to break through into France.

SIX

AGES OF FAITH

THE Middle Ages (roughly 1000-1500 AD) are sometimes called 'ages of faith'. In western Europe, Church and state were closely linked, while the Pope became the political ruler of a large part of central Italy – the 'Papal States'. Great churches and cathedrals were built, many of which stand to this day. Humble believers would go on pilgrimage: to seek healing from St Thomas à Becket at Canterbury in England, or from St James at Compostella in Spain. Some monastic orders lost their zeal for holy living – but new ones were founded. Education and some medical knowledge were encouraged.

To the ordinary believer, non-Christians were far away, apart from the Jewish minority who were often wrongly blamed for the death of Jesus. All too often the Jews were persecuted, wrongly suspected and cruelly victimised or even massacred. Jews were expelled from England in 1290 and from Spain in 1492. Many moved east, to Poland, where their descendants lived until the Second World War.

The Crusades
By the 11th century, Christendom had recovered from the Arab onslaught and many Christians thought it right to fight back. The Crusades were launched, with the great goal of recapturing the lost lands where the Christian faith was born. In 1099 the warriors of the First Crusade succeeded in recapturing – in their terms, liberating – the holy city of Jerusalem. Sadly, they celebrated their victory with a massacre.

But did not Jesus say, 'Love your enemies'? Some thought that Christian warfare should be fought only with the sword of the Spirit. The Christian philosopher Roger Bacon wrote in 1268: 'When Christians discuss matters with pagans the latter are easily won over. They would become Christians very gladly but the princes who labour for their conversion desire to reduce them to slavery.'

Roger Bacon was thinking of a mission to the tribes of eastern Europe, whose temple to Svantovit – a god with four faces – stood on the island of Rügen (now in Germany). But other Christians thought differently. To them Svantovit looked like the devil in disguise. Was it not right – even a duty – to declare a crusade, invade the idol's country and destroy Satan's temple? This happened in 1107. Missionaries could then move in and preach the gospel to the misguided people.

Such crusades succeeded in northern Europe but failed in the eastern world. By 1291 the last crusader state was lost, and local Christians were left to survive as minority communities under a succession of Islamic rulers.

The ideals of Christendom
In the fusion of Church and state in western Europe – sometimes called 'Christendom' – new ideas developed which were to influence the thinking of later ages.

Romantic love
The Church struggled to civilise the violent sexual impulses of the peoples of Europe and to encourage Christian marriage. In the 11th century there arose the cult of romantic love. Starting in Provence in the south of France (formerly called the Roman Province of Gaul – hence 'Romantic') popular singers spread the ideal of passionate love between a noble knight and a beautiful young lady – who might perhaps have been forced into an arranged marriage. The Church stood for 'one man-one wife', but was against forced marriage.

Slowly a compromise developed. Christian couples should first be passionately attracted to each other ('in love') but they should wait to get married and then be faithful to each other ever afterwards. Thus there grew up the ideal of 'romantic love' which inspired many people in Europe, and elsewhere, until it was largely overthrown by the sexual revolution of the 1960s.

The code of chivalry

Europe's culture glorified the fighting soldier – the 'knight'. Originally a member of the king's war band, the medieval knight was expected to obey the code of chivalry. This required knights to fight fairly, protect women and children, and spare the lives of prisoners. In the 15th century the poet Stephen Hawes expressed the chivalrous ideal:

> For knighthood is not in the feats of war,
> As for to fight in quarrel – right or wrong –
> But in a cause which truth does not debar
> He ought to make himself both sure and strong.

Sometimes the code of chivalry was effective but all too often knights degenerated into thugs. One young man, though, was to turn himself into a 'knight of peace' – a champion and friend of the poor.

Francis of Assisi (1182-1226) was a happy young man from a well-to-do Italian family. He was looking forward to a career as a fighting knight until he was taken prisoner in a local war. Then he fell ill and was warned in a vision to become a new soldier of Christ. But how? Francis was not sure. His first attempt was to rebuild a ruined church in his native Assisi.

Then, like St Antony before him, Francis heard the words of Jesus: 'Sell all you have and give to the poor.' These he took as a commandment to him personally. Francis shocked his father by giving away all his possessions, wearing rough clothes and preaching a gospel of purity and peace. Leaving home dressed in a ragged cloak, he wandered through the countryside begging from

39

the rich and giving to the poor – and sharing the good news with everyone. His kindness and sincerity attracted many followers.

Many stories were told about Francis. He is said to have preached to the birds and to have converted a fierce wolf which terrorised the village of Gubbio. Thanks to Francis's preaching, Brother Wolf became tame and came to live as a friend of the villagers.

Behind these stories is the figure of a man who took the teaching of Jesus literally, visiting hospitals and caring for lepers. He saw the whole of creation as his 'brothers and sisters' – for all had God as their father.

Francis applied for permission from the Pope to set up a new Christian society. Soon they were formed into a fellowship – the Friars Minor (Lesser Brothers). Francis was joined by Clare, his spiritual student, whose followers and spiritual sisters were known as the 'Poor Clares'.

With growth in numbers came problems. Who was to look after the money that people gave to them? How could the Friars help the poor if they did not own property? Some structure was needed. In 1223 a new rule was authorised by the Pope, allowing for a more elaborate organisation.

Francis was distressed. He felt the new order was not what Christ had commanded him. 'I have worked with my hands,' he wrote in his *Testament*, 'and I want all my other brethren to work at an honest craft.'

Francis resigned and went into retreat in the mountains. Here, while engaged in fervent prayer, he received strange marks in his hands – stigmata – which sometimes bled during the last two years of his life. During his last illness, while resting in the convent of his friend and helper Clare, Francis composed his 'Hymn of Creation', using simple Italian, not official Latin, which has been described as 'the most beautiful religious poetry since the gospels':

> *All creatures of our God and King*
> *Lift up your voice and with us sing*
> *Alleluia.*

As death drew near he added the words:

> And thou most kind and gentle death
> Thou leadest home the child of God,
> And Christ our Lord the way hath trod.

(trs William Henry Draper)

Keeping the flame of faith alive

Like many of the great religious and monastic orders, the Friars were tempted to lose their spiritual ideals. In the following century the English poet Geoffrey Chaucer poked fun at the cheerful, worldly, begging Friar of his own day. Unlike Francis, Chaucer's Friar kept clear of people who suffered from leprosy, but was very willing to tell people their sins were forgiven, in return for a donation:

> If prayers and weeping fill your soul with dread
> Why not give silver to the Friars instead?

But nothing could destroy the appeal of St Francis – God's poor little saint – and soon the question of 'cheap forgiveness' would be debated with such passion that the western Church would be split apart.

Moscow the Third Rome

Should the Church sell all it possessed, or did it need land and organisation? Such questions were also asked in Russia, where Eastern Orthodox Christianity was gaining strength. The Eastern Roman Empire came to an end in 1453, when the Muslim Turks captured Constantinople, but soon afterwards the Grand Duke of Muscovy took the title 'Tsar' (Caesar). 'Two Romes have fallen,' declared the monk Philotheos. 'The third – Moscow – stands and there will be no fourth. In all the world you are the only Christian Tsar.'

This meant that the Russian Orthodox Church came to be closely allied with the Russian state. Peasants were becoming serfs, tied to the land. So if the monastery owned land, the monks might have to order the flogging of a peasant.

Many Christians argued, like Francis, that the Church should not own property, land or wealth of any kind. The Russians called them **'non-possessors'**. They were led by the saintly Nilus of Sorsk. Some sought freedom by working as hermits or missionaries on the expanding Russian frontier far from Moscow. Cyril of Novoyezersk survived on bark, roots and grass, and lived among wild beasts for 20 years.

But how could the Church hope to feed the poor if it had no food, and no barns to store the food in? This was the argument of the **'possessors'** led by Joseph of the monastery of Volokolamsk, not far from Moscow. His case seemed stronger, and the Russian Church proclaimed him a saint. The other side was not forgotten and Nilus was declared a saint too – but only shortly before the Revolution of 1917, which overthrew the Tsar and destroyed the Church's political power.

SEVEN

THE REFORMATION

BY the year 1500 the western Church was plainly in need of renewal. It had become closely linked to the world. For example, a king might appoint his own illegitimate son to be an archbishop. Church positions were sold and the revenues often diverted to the state. This was the sin of 'simony', named after Simon Magus, who tried to buy the Holy Spirit from Peter (Acts 8:18). It could be combined with 'pluralism', which meant holding several Church posts at once and receiving all the salaries. Churchmen also held top government jobs which did not agree with their spiritual calling. Notorious was Cardinal Wolsey, Chancellor to King Henry VIII of England. As he lay dying, Wolsey lamented, if only 'I had served God as well as I have served my king'.

At the head of the western Church stood the Pope, in Rome. He was now a political as well as a religious leader, ruling over a large region of central Italy known as the Papal States. This meant he needed an army. In 1517 Pope Julius II led his troops into battle, dressed in full armour.

Much popular superstition had become mixed with the gospel. People were encouraged to put their trust in the relics of saints, which were believed to have healing power. But this gave plenty of opportunity for cheating. The poet Geoffrey Chaucer's list of medieval rascals includes a 'pardoner' who claims to have a piece of the sail from Peter's fishing boat.

There was also the problem of first- and second-class Christianity. Ordinary believers were often felt to be on a lower spiritual level than monks, priests and nuns who were called to obey 'counsels of perfection'.

A further abuse was over the doctrine of purgatory. People believed that the righteous would go straight to Heaven after death, and the hopelessly wicked to hell. But many sinners not yet fit for Heaven would spend time in purgatory – a place of painful purification.

It was natural to be concerned for the souls of those who had died, so people would pray for the release of their loved ones from purgatory. The Church was thought to have built up a bank of goodness – a 'treasury of merit' – which could be applied to help those in purgatory.

In 1527 Pope Julius – he of the suit of armour – was planning to rebuild the great cathedral of St Peter's in Rome. Money was needed, so an 'indulgence' was proclaimed. A Pardoner – Tetzel – went on tour in Germany, declaring that those who bought an indulgence or gave a donation could be sure that their loved one was set free from purgatory. Tetzel's preaching declared:

> *As soon as the penny goes clink in the chest*
> *The soul flies up to its Heavenly rest.*

The dispute about indulgences began the Reformation which left the western Church divided into Roman Catholics and Protestants.

Martin Luther's protest
Among those shocked by Tetzel's preaching was a young monk called Martin Luther (1483-1546). Luther was born the son of a prosperous miner. He felt called to become a monk, and entered a community of faithful Christians where the rule was faithfully kept. He was also a man of the people, filling his sermons with entertaining stories. He searched for spiritual guidance while giving lectures on the writings of Paul, and summed up his understanding by stressing the text: 'The righteous will live by faith' (Romans 1:17). You could not please a gracious God by non-

stop praying or by sticking to rules, but true repentance and simple trust would set you free.

Luther was horrified when he heard about the activities of Tetzel. He drafted numerous points for debate (the **Ninety-five Theses**) and nailed them to the church door in the university city of Wittenberg. Indulgences, he declared, were a denial of the gospel. If the Pope had power to release souls from purgatory, why not release them all at once?

But still the sale of indulgences was authorised by the Pope, the successor of Peter and head of the Universal Church! Luther's critics pressed him hard. If you are against indulgences you are also against the authority of the Holy Father! Which is it to be?

Soon Germany was on fire with argument. Thanks to the new invention of printing, Luther's writings – composed in a plain and punchy style – were widely read. In the year 1520 he published three pamphlets. One of them was titled *To the Christian Nobility of the German Nation*. Luther compared it to the blast of the trumpet which brought down the walls of Jericho. The German princes must break the power of the Pope in Germany. They must abolish indulgences and encourage a simpler Christianity based on the Bible. The Pope issued a Bull (official edict) condemning Luther. In reply Luther burnt a copy of it and threw the ashes into the River Elbe. Now there could be no going back.

The Emperor of Germany (known as the 'Holy Roman Emperor') summoned Luther to a state meeting, the Diet (Council) of Worms. This was dangerous. When an earlier reformer, Jan Hus, attended a similar meeting a century before this he was betrayed and burnt alive.

Luther decided to go to the meeting. Rejecting the claims of the papacy, he appealed to the authority of the Bible. 'Unless I am proved wrong by Scripture,' he said, 'I am a prisoner in conscience to the word of God.' Tradition declares that he added the famous words: 'Here I stand. I can do no other.'

Luther's life was spared. Back in his native Saxony, in hiding at Wartburg Castle, Luther began translating the Bible into German.

He also wrote hymns. Deciding that the celibacy rule was wrong, he gave up life as a monk and married Katherine von Bora, a former nun. 'I would not change my Katie for France and Venice,' he said.

A Church divided: Roman Catholics and Protestants

Now the Church was divided. Many of Luther's old friends thought he had gone too far. They stayed faithful to the Pope, hoping to reform the Church from within. But others thought Luther had not gone far enough. Why did he depend on the wealthy German princes for support? Were the princes any better than the Pope? What about the struggling peasants?

In 1525 the peasants rose in rebellion, demanding political as well as religious freedom. Some ran wild and committed atrocities, spearing the Count of Helfenstein to death in front of his family.

In reply to such misdeeds Luther wrote a disastrous pamphlet, *Against the Murdering Hordes of Peasants*. The historian Owen Chadwick tells us that he imagined a brave citizen standing up to a mob of rioters but by the time the pamphlet appeared the peasants had been defeated and were being hunted down by the revenging overlords.

The Lutheran Church

Luther believed that every believer was free in Christ, which meant that two-tier Christianity had to go. But he loved the old ways of the Church and wanted to alter as little as possible. Luther thought it right to keep any custom that is not plainly forbidden in the Bible. That is why the appearance and worship of a Lutheran Church seems rather similar to that of a Roman Catholic Church. Luther also loved music. He himself composed and sang. In later centuries the Lutheran Church would produce great Christian composers, including Johann Sebastian Bach and G. F. Handel. So, indirectly, we owe the 'Hallelujah Chorus' to Martin Luther.

Europe divided

European Christendom was now divided. In 1529 a group of Luther's supporters made a declaration of support (a 'Protest') in his favour. Thus arose the name 'Protestant'. Those who continued to accept the authority of the Pope were the 'Roman Catholics' – often called 'Catholics' for short.

Most people still thought that there could be only one true religion in any state. But which one was it to be? In Germany the local rulers agreed on the rule, *Cuius regio – eius religio* ('Whose region? His religion!'). The prince or duke should decide between Roman Catholicism and Protestantism. Those who did not like it could migrate to another principality where their own version of the faith was practised.

But this could not be a long-term answer to the problem of religious toleration.

Calvin and Calvinism

The name 'Protestant' was applied to a number of Reformers, none more influential than the Frenchman John Calvin (1509-1564). Less passionate than Luther, Calvin was a clear and cool thinker who looked to the Bible to discover Christian truth. Forced out of France, he went to live in French-speaking Geneva (part of Switzerland) where he tried, with others, to set up a true Christian commonwealth.

If Luther's message was 'By faith alone', Calvin's motto was 'To God alone the glory!' His profound and logical ideas were expressed in his *Institutes*, a handbook of doctrine beautifully written in both French and Latin. Many eager spirits were convinced by his clear and persuasive teaching. They came to be known as 'Reformed' Protestants.

Luther taught that you could retain any custom not forbidden in Scripture. Calvin believed you should do only what was *expressed* in Scripture. So the worship of the reformed churches was simple and austere. There were no hymns, only biblical psalms in rhyming verse. There was no place for organs or other musical instruments either. At the heart of worship lay the preaching of the word – the sermon – so the pulpit replaced the altar as the centre of reformed worship.

Rejecting the claims of the Pope, Calvin looked to the Bible for a plan of Church government. He believed that Scripture taught a system of Church administration by leading elders (presbyters) and ordained ministers. The prince (or king) had no right to appoint Church leaders or interfere with the running of the Church. In extreme cases, the Church might support the overthrow of a bad king.

Calvin's teaching on Church government was controversial. Was the Presbyterian system really to be found in the New Testament? Also questionable was his teaching on 'double predestination' – stating that God had decided from all eternity who should be saved and who should go to hell. Calvin called this the *decretum horribile* – 'the terrible decree'. Many disagreed. 'I am not predestinated,' declared a critic, 'whatever you … may say.'

In France, and elsewhere in Europe, the Calvinists remained a minority. Only in Scotland did Calvin's disciple – John Knox – succeed in setting up a reformed church as close as possible to Calvin's plan. This soon led to conflict with the king, for the Reformed Church refused to accept royal control.

'There are two kings in Scotland,' said church leader Andrew Melville. 'One is King James and the other is King Jesus.' King James VI was unhappy. He thought God had given him power to rule by Divine Right.

England and Anglicanism: 'The Middle Way'

In England, King Henry VIII began by attacking Martin Luther's teaching, for which the Pope gave him the title 'Defender of the Faith', which the British monarch bears to this day.

But Henry was desperate for a son, and his wife Queen Catherine had borne him only a daughter. Henry turned against the papacy, which forbade his divorce, sacked his Chancellor, Cardinal Wolsey, and made himself 'Supreme Governor' of the Church of

England. He also forced a brutal closure of the historic monasteries. But much of the traditional Roman Catholic practice remained, as did government by bishops. Thus the Church of England has sought to offer a 'middle way' between Rome (the Roman Catholics) and Geneva (the Protestants).

Some English Christians were unhappy. They wanted a more 'Protestant' Church of England. Because of their strict principles, they were nicknamed 'Puritans'. And when, in 1603, King James of Scotland inherited the English throne, he regarded them with suspicion. James believed he ruled by Divine Right and suspected the Puritans might one day turn into rebels. His policy was, 'No bishop – no king'.

The radicals of the Reformation

Roman Catholics thought Luther and Calvin had gone too far. Others thought they had not gone far enough. There were further questions to be asked. Is it scriptural to baptise babies who are not old enough to express personal faith? Should the Church not wait until believers are old enough to decide for themselves? Those who rejected infant baptism were called Anabaptists. Should Christians take part in war? Luther taught that a soldier could be a faithful Christian. But did not Jesus say, 'Love your enemies'? Surely the 'code of chivalry' was humbug?

Why have any state Church at all? Both Luther and Calvin – like the Roman Catholics – believed ministers or priests should be paid, at least in part, out of public funds. Where was the Scripture for that? If church attendance was compulsory by law, as school attendance is in many countries nowadays, on Sunday the village church might be filled with half-hearted, inattentive people. Where was the Scripture for that? Surely any group of true believers meeting in the name of Jesus could form a church, elect their own pastor and support him by voluntary donations. Could 'him' even be 'her'? There were even calls for women's ministry.

This seemed absurd in an age when social welfare was provided by the Church not the state. The proposals of the radicals looked like plans for chaos and they were cruelly persecuted. In Switzerland, Anabaptists were drowned in Lake Zurich. There was a grim saying: 'Those who "dipped" others should themselves be "dipped" (drowned).'

More shocking still were questions about the doctrine of the Trinity. Was it truly scriptural? Faustus Socinus (1539-1604) – who questioned the divinity of Jesus – found refuge in Poland, where his Unitarian (Socinian) teaching spread among the upper classes. But for many Christian believers his teaching was too much. Socinus published his works anonymously, but when his identity became known a mob rioted and he was forced to flee the city of Krakow.

Thus the Reformation led to spiritual renewal, but also to conflict. Nevertheless its effects were to resound around the world, and the divisions in today's international Church still reflect the debates of the Reformation period.

EIGHT

THE COUNTER-REFORMATION

The faith is carried east and west

THE Reformation left the western Church divided into Protestants and Roman Catholics – a division which has continued to the present day. But while many Christians followed the Reformers, others continued to seek renewal from within. This led to the 'Counter-Reformation', restoring the spiritual strength of the Roman Catholic Church and sending its missionaries around the world.

The Council of Trent

Many Church leaders called for a general Church Council to deal with the challenge of the reformers, and if possible reach agreement. But when the Council of Trent finally met (in northern Italy, from 1545-63) it only confirmed the split that had already taken place. Protestants wanted the Bible to be translated into local languages, but the Council declared that the Latin version of the Bible (itself a translation of the Hebrew and Greek originals) was the sacred and canonical text. Protestant pastors and ministers were allowed to marry, but the Council declared that Roman Catholic priests must remain single. Protestants wanted all believers to receive both bread and wine in Holy Communion – but the Council decreed that they should continue to partake of the bread only, with the priest receiving the wine. Disagreements over the mysterious presence of the Lord Jesus in Holy Communion proved impossible to resolve.

Sadly, it soon became clear that there would be no reconciliation between Roman Catholic and Protestant – instead the Roman Catholic Church would do its best to put its own house in order.

A renewed papacy

Reform had to begin at the very top, with the Pope himself. There was no room now for corrupt and worldly leadership. 'It would be almost unthinkable,' wrote the historian Owen Chadwick, 'for the Pope of 1459 to be elected in 1559.' Pius V (Pope from 1565-72) was a man of faith and great self denial. He declared that the Church had no need of soldiers, for its weapons were prayer and fasting, tears and the Bible. Strict in his own personal life and strict with others, he was a man of great charity, but nevertheless in favour of the persecution of Protestants, and even wanting to impose the death penalty for adultery.

Gone west!

Just as the Roman Catholic Church lost ground in Europe, new fields of mission opened up across the ocean. In 1492 the explorer Christopher Columbus reached the West Indies. Later explorers pressed on to the American mainland and soon an entire continent was open to colonisation by Spain and Portugal.

In the early days of conquest the soldier had more power than the preacher. Many of the victorious Spaniards were little better than thugs. When the Inca of Peru was captured (1521) he was asked to accept the Christian religion and submit to the King of Spain. He refused, whereupon Spaniards, emerging from hiding, slaughtered several thousand Peruvians.

Nevertheless, some of the Spanish 'conquistadors' sincerely felt they were doing God's work. The ghastly human sacrifices practised by the Aztecs in Mexico City looked like the work of Satan himself! Was it not right to smash idols, knock down temples and build Christian churches on the foundations?

The debate about human rights

Such was the argument of the theologian Sepulveda, who held that it was a Christian duty to first conquer the Indians, and then convert them. But he was opposed by Bartholomew de Las Casas, the first priest to be ordained in the new world. In the year 1550 Sepulveda and Las Casas argued the case in a memorable debate before the King of Spain.

Las Casas had already been campaigning to defend the rights of Native Americans. War, he said, was no way to spread the gospel. Conquerors who claimed to be defending the Church were really after loot. People should be brought to Christ through peaceful preaching and holy living. Here he got support from the Pope himself, who declared it was wrong to make slaves out of the Indians, as the Native Americans were called.

The Church of the Counter-Reformation tried hard to share the faith with the American peoples. Missionaries often relied on mass baptism – one reported that 14,000 people were baptised in one day. This produced huge numbers of nominal Christians who had only a vague understanding of the gospel.

Missionaries also attempted to protect the native peoples by organising them into safe villages. Las Casas tried it on the island of Puerto Rico but his model society collapsed in civil war with Spanish settlers. Later on, Jesuit missionaries (see below) did their best to protect the native peoples from incoming colonists by providing them with secure reservations where they could live in peace and learn the faith.

Thus the work of the Counter-Reformation turned much of South America into a continent of strongly Roman Catholic faith. But it had one weakness. Native peoples were often protected but too often were treated like children. For nearly 300 years there were no Native American priests. The first three were ordained in the year 1794.

The Jesuits

Leading the missionary work of the Counter-Reformation was a new religious fellowship, the 'Society of Jesus', or Jesuits. Its founder – Ignatius Loyola (1491-1556) – was a Spanish soldier who turned his talent to spiritual warfare after a war wound crippled him in the leg. Like Martin Luther he tried fasting and self denial and wrote a famous handbook on prayer, *Spiritual Exercises*. In 1534 he gathered a group of six men and applied to the Pope for permission to set up a new religious order. At last, in 1540, the Society of Jesus came into being. Ignatius wanted his community to be active, serving the heathen, helping the poor and giving Christian education to the illiterate. Unlike other religious orders, the Jesuits were not expected to meet together for communal daily worship. The Jesuits were to be spiritual soldiers of Christ.

The voyage to the east

One of the original six was Francis Xavier. In 1541 he set sail with three other Jesuits for the Far East. He landed in Goa, then a Portuguese town, on the coast of India. The Christian faith had been brought to India many centuries before, traditionally by the apostle Thomas. Now a new world mission had begun.

As with Francis of Assisi, legends surround the life of Francis Xavier. He used interpreters to translate the Lord's Prayer, the Creed and the Ten Commandments. 'On Sunday,' he wrote, 'I assemble all the people, men and women, young and old, and we get them to repeat the prayers in their language.'

But Francis Xavier was not content to stay in India. In 1549 he reached Japan and was very pleased at what he found. He declared: 'We shall never find among heathens another race to equal the Japanese.'

China, too, possessed a proud and ancient civilisation. Here the Jesuit Matteo Ricci (1552-1610) gained the favour of the Emperor and impressed the Chinese by his scientific knowledge. His book *The True Doctrine of God*, written in Chinese, was to be used by generations of missionaries. Ricci went a long way in adapting the Christian faith, attempting, for example, to make space for Chinese reverence for ancestors. Some thought he had gone too far, and after his death the Pope ruled against him.

Similar problems were faced in Japan. Unlike the peoples of South America, the Chinese and Japanese already had a strong society and an efficient system of writing. They had to be persuaded, not conquered. But how far should the Christian faith go in adapting to their culture and customs? What was the right Japanese word for 'God'? Should missionaries wear cotton (the dress of the poor) or silk (the clothing of the rich)? Francis of Assisi would, no doubt, have chosen cotton, but a leading Jesuit – Alessandro Valignano – ruled in favour of silk, for this would allow missionaries to gain access to the influential people. In this they often succeeded. He also decided that Japanese Christians could become priests. The first four were ordained in the year 1601, and one of them – Sebastian Chimura – was to die a martyr in 1622.

The Christian mission seemed to be prospering, with an estimated 300,000 Japanese Christians. But some suspected it was part of a foreign takeover. In 1614 the Shogun (ruler) issued a grim decree: 'The Christian band have come to Japan ... to overthrow true doctrine so that they may ... obtain possession of the land. This is the germ of a great disaster and must be crushed.'

A fearful persecution broke out. In 24 years about 1,900 believers died a martyr's death, of whom 62 were European missionaries. For two centuries Japan remained seemingly closed to the gospel, although time would show that a tiny remnant of Christians remained, whose descendants greeted the missionaries who returned more than two centuries later.

NINE

FAITH, HOPE AND CONFLICT

Great Britain and Ireland in the 17th century

'They called my father Puritan'
WHILE Christians in Japan were facing cruel torture for their faith, a young boy called Richard Baxter was sitting in a country church in faraway England, feeling bored. The service was based on the Church of England's *Book of Common Prayer*, but the leader was a blind man, 80 years old, who said the words from memory. There was no sermon and the Scriptures were read by a poorly qualified farm labourer. As soon as the service was over, the villagers began to relax by dancing the morris – the traditional folk dance of the English people (Sunday was their only day off work).

For Richard Baxter's father this was not good enough. He thought Sunday should be kept holy as the Lord's Day, and he supplemented half-hearted morning church with household prayers in the afternoon. But soon the Bible study was disturbed by the loud music of the pipe and tabor (a kind of one-man band).

More than once young Richard was tempted to leave the Bible study and run away to join the dancers outside. But he soon returned home, for some of the revellers sneered at his beloved parent. Years later he wrote in his journal: 'When they called my father "Puritan" I considered that our way was better than theirs.' Richard's long life, faithfully lived through strife and turmoil, takes us through the 17th century.

The Baxter afternoon Bible study was the beginning of a split. The mass of the people were attending the parish church – still compulsory by law – while a committed minority met as a house group. But such groups could easily turn into breakaway or independent churches.

This was all the more likely because the 17th century was an age of passionate **Bible study**. People had learnt to read, and printing had made the Bible available to them. Many searched the word but not all agreed as to what it meant. Some thought it contained political as well as spiritual truth, so that a modern state should be re-modelled on the lines of ancient Judah.

It was also the great age of **Psalm singing**. In line with the teaching of Calvin, the Psalms had been turned into rhyming verse by Thomas Sternhold and John Hopkins. Their poetry was poor but popular. The Puritans had some good melodies of their own to compete with the pipe-and-tabor player. Two of their best tunes, 'The Old Hundredth' and 'Winchester Old', are still widely sung today.

It was an age of **preaching** and the great preachers were popular and entertaining teachers. That is why Richard Baxter's father was so dissatisfied with the old blind reader who never preached a sermon. And since church attendance was compulsory, at least in theory, a preacher could reach as big an audience as a local radio station does nowadays. No wonder the government was wary of preachers. Books, pamphlets and the newly invented newspapers could all be censored by the state, but it was hard to stop people from speaking their mind in the pulpit.

Richard Baxter's father was mocked as a Puritan – a strict and narrow-minded Christian. But how strict was strict? Puritans objected to the theatre – on which they may well have been wrong – but they also opposed the cruel sport of bear baiting, on which they were right. 'What Christian heart,' wrote one of them, 'can take pleasure to see one poor beast rend, tear and kill another?'

Many so-called Puritans – like Richard's father – cared passionately about their God and their country, and worked for reform in Church and state. But who was to have the final say in religious matters?

The Pope, the Prince and the Presbytery

For Roman Catholics the ultimate authority was the Pope. But Roman Catholicism was officially banned throughout the three Kingdoms of England, Scotland and Ireland. The Roman Catholic faith continued 'underground' in England and also 'above ground' where the government's writ did not run. In Ireland and parts of Scotland the Roman Catholic faith still held the loyalty of most of the people and was sustained by semi-independent Lords and Chiefs.

The Protestants had replaced the Pope with the Bible – but who was to interpret it? Could not the Devil quote Scripture for his own purpose? For many earnest Christians in the Puritan camp, the final authority was the **presbytery** – the system of Church government based on the New Testament as interpreted by Calvin. Just such a church had been set up in Scotland.

But King James, who had moved to London after inheriting the English throne, believed the last word must lie with the Prince (that is to say, the King). As King of England and Supreme Governor of the Church he claimed to rule by Divine Right. He could not define Christian truth or change Christian doctrine but he did have the duty to appoint Church leaders (the bishops).

And what of those who could accept neither Pope, prince nor presbytery? They should either keep quiet or leave the country.

The Pilgrim Fathers

Indeed, small groups of separatists had already left the Anglican Church and gone to live in The Netherlands. There they set up independent churches based on personal commitment. Back home, many regarded them as humbugs and hypocrites. The dramatist Ben Jonson – a friend of Shakespeare – lampooned their leader as 'Ananias', after the cheat who tried to deceive the apostles (Acts 5:1-6).

Then in 1620 a little band set sail for America aboard *The Mayflower*. They hoped to form a new settlement based on Christian principles. Their leader, John Robinson, told them to

59

shake off 'the odious name of Puritan'. He told them: 'God hath yet more light to break from his holy word.'

The Pilgrim Fathers (as they came to be known) were followed by other settlers who established settlements which are now part of the United States of America. In 1630 the **Massachusetts Bay Company** established a new society based on Puritan ideals. They did not intend to set up a religious free-for-all. In their new Commonwealth, only church members were allowed to vote.

Meanwhile on the other side of the Atlantic King Charles I had succeeded King James as ruler of three kingdoms – England, Scotland and Ireland – each of which experienced a different form of Christianity. Most people thought that only one of them could be right. A conflict of words and ideas was soon to turn into a war of pikes and muskets.

The War of the Three Kingdoms

The War of the Three Kingdoms began in 1638, when King Charles – based in London – tried to impose an Anglican form of worship on the Church of Scotland. In reply many Scots signed a pledge (covenant) to defend the Reformed Church as described by Calvin. For them the head of the Church was not King Charles but King Jesus. Scottish battle flags were embellished with the words 'For Christ's Crown and Covenant'. The Reformed Church – they held – should be set up throughout the Three Kingdoms of England Scotland and Ireland. As Ireland in particular was strongly Roman Catholic, this was an unlikely dream indeed. But few Christians at that time could accept the idea of different churches in the same country.

Richard Baxter hears the guns firing

Soon the civil war spread to England, Wales and Ireland. In 1642 Richard Baxter – now a respected parish minister – was preaching at Alcester in the English midlands. Halfway through his sermon the congregation became restless. They could hear a distant rumbling sound. Forty miles away, on the field of Edgehill, great guns were firing. On the following day Richard visited the site and saw more than 1,000 dead bodies lying on the field.

Reform or revolution?

As the tide of war turned against King Charles, the Scottish Covenanters and their English allies were dismayed by the revolutionary ideas that were brewing in the parliamentary army. They were most extreme among the cavalry, led by the dynamic Oliver Cromwell (1599-1658). The Covenanters were horrified when Cromwell refused to sack 'Anabaptist' soldiers. 'They are godly, sober Christians,' he declared.

Oliver's horsemen were all volunteers committed to 'godly reformation in church and state'. As Christian soldiers, they formed themselves into a 'gathered church'. They wanted a well-qualified pastor to guide them, and invited the much-respected Richard Baxter to fill the post.

Richard was flattered, for Cromwell's men were 'so valiant, they never ran away from any'. But he was also shocked, for independent 'gathered' churches would mean the end of the inclusive parish system. It might even begin the break-up of 'Christian England' as he understood it.

He wrote back, 'reproving' their attempt to form a breakaway congregation. But soon he had second thoughts, for the English Parliament's army was alive with new, shocking and revolutionary ideas.

The Independents and Anabaptists

The **Independents** believed that each local church should be self-governing and that various forms of Protestant Christianity should be allowed. The **Anabaptists** agreed about Church government but rejected the baptism of infants as unscriptural.

Even more alarming were the **Levellers,** who wanted one-man-one-vote while the **True Levellers** or **Diggers** thought the land of

England should be taken away from the wealthy and divided up among the people. They started digging on common land but were soon dispersed.

The **Fifth Monarchy Men** believed that Christ's return would follow the overthrow of King Charles, the 'Man of Blood'. They got this theory from intense study of the Book of Daniel, chapter 12. Among them was Thomas Harrison, one of the bravest – and most deluded – of the parliamentary soldiers.

Stranger still were the **Muggletonians**, who believed that two soldiers in the parliamentary army – Muggleton and Reeve – were the two witnesses promised in Revelation 11:6. The last member of the Muggletonian sect died in 1971.

The **Ranters** were the 'hippies' of the age. They went in for tobacco smoking (like cannabis today) and sexual freedom, holding that 'all things come by nature'. Not many of them joined the God-fearing army. But 300 years later, when 'sex, drugs and rock-and-roll' became popular, the Ranters would be praised as pioneers

More long-lasting was the **Society of Friends,** whose members Richard Baxter thought were 'the Ranters turned from horrid … blasphemy to a life of extreme austerity on the other side'. Inspired by the teaching of George Fox (1624-91), the Friends rejected all formal worship, referring to church buildings as 'steeple houses'. They refused to swear oaths (in accordance, they believed, with Matthew 5:34) and came to renounce all war. The Friends placed the guidance of the Holy Spirit above Scripture, stressing the importance of the 'Inner Light' within the soul. They also rejected showy clothes and ultra-polite ways of speaking. Most shocking was their abandonment of the two sacraments of water baptism and the Lord's Supper.

The Friends also rejected the idea of a paid professional ministry, for God had revealed to George Fox that he did not need to be 'bred up at Oxford or Cambridge' (universities) to preach the gospel. Men *and* women were free to speak in Friends' worship meetings.

Friends often shook or quaked under the influence of the Spirit, thereby gaining the nickname 'Quakers', which like 'Christian' and 'Methodist' became a badge of honour.

George Scott Railton – The Salvation Army's first commissioner – saw The Salvation Army in its early days as a revival of the pioneering Quakers, whom he called 'George Fox and his Salvation Army 200 years ago'!

Freedom of conscience for all?

Most believers still thought there could be only one Church. You could not allow people to go around spreading 'wrong ideas'. Those who could not put up with the official religion should keep quiet or emigrate. But government censorship had broken down, and many revolutionary pamphlets were published.

One was written by Roger Williams (1604-1683), who had gone to America in search of religious freedom. But he was expelled from Massachusetts and began a new settlement in Rhode Island, nowadays also one of the United States. When war broke out on the other side of the Atlantic he returned to England and published *The Bloody Tenent* (Law) *of Persecution for Cause of Conscience Displayed.*

He wrote: 'God requireth not an uniformity of religion to be enacted in any civil state ... True civility and Christianity may both flourish in a state or kingdom, notwithstanding the permission of divers and contrary consciences.'

In calling for religious toleration – as in his friendship with Native Americans – Roger Williams was a true 'pioneer of the spirit', for what may seem obvious now did not seen obvious then.

The English Republic

In 1649 the defeated King Charles was put on trial and executed. He went to his death bravely. 'I have a just God and a gracious Saviour,' he said. His supporters honoured him as 'King Charles the Martyr'.

Oliver Cromwell emerged as Lord Protector of the triumphant English republic. He genuinely believed in liberty of conscience, within limits, and allowed Jews to return to England. His regime was prepared to cooperate with various new Protestant sects. Richard Baxter reluctantly admitted that under his rule England could have become 'a land of saints and a pattern of holiness to all the world'.

But things were tragically very different in mainly Roman Catholic Ireland. Roman Catholics could believe what they liked but Cromwell declared that, 'No one would say mass wherever the parliament of England had power.' The spread of Protestantism had got mixed up with an English land grab. 'The curse of Cromwell be on you!' became an Irish saying.

In fact 'the curse of Cromwell' was really 'the curse of England' and it continued long after the Protector's death. A generation later Sir Neil O'Neill, one of the last independent Irish chiefs, had his portrait painted. In it he stands defiant, wearing traditional Irish dress, with an Irish wolfhound at his side. Beside him lies a suit of Japanese armour. Sir Neil was comparing the sufferings of Roman Catholics in Ireland with those in Japan.

O'Neill perished at the Battle of the Boyne in 1690, defending his homeland against an army of Protestants, many of whom had been forced by persecution to leave their native France.

The king's return: John Bunyan in jail

In 1660, after Cromwell's death, the English Republic collapsed and in 1660 King Charles II returned. Religious conformity was reimposed. The government invited the much-respected Richard Baxter to accept royal appointment as a bishop but he refused and was evicted from his Church post along with thousands of others. Many went to jail, among them the Baptist preacher John Bunyan (1626-1688) – a former soldier in the parliamentary army.

While in prison, Bunyan wrote his classic book *The Pilgrim's Progress*. He also drew on his wartime memories to compose *The*

Holy War between Immanuel (Christ) and Diabolus (Satan). Horsemen and footmen appear in the great struggle between good and evil. Here – if anywhere – is the origin of the military symbolism taken over by The Salvation Army 200 years later.

Others suffered an even worse fate. Thomas Harrison – the Fifth Monarchy Man – was brutally put to death. He had been wrong about the date of the Second Coming but he died with great courage. At his trial he quoted words from the apostle Paul: 'These things were not done in a corner.'

Harrison was right. The War of the Three Kingdoms, and the ferment of religious and political ideas that went with it, were to have huge influence on the Christian Church, especially in the English-speaking world.

Richard Baxter looks back

Richard Baxter lived on to endure further persecution. Towards the end of his life he looked back and wondered how his mind had changed. First, as to Roman Catholics. As a young man he had been persuaded that no Roman Catholic could be saved. Since they did not have true faith, all would go to hell. But as an older man he declared: 'I doubt not that God hath many sanctified ones among them ... I can never believe that God will cast a soul into hell that truly loveth him.'

Then there was the call to overseas mission. Too much time had been wasted on internal conflict. 'I was wont to look but little further than England in my prayers ... but now no part of my prayers are so deeply serious as that for the conversion of the infidel and ungodly world,' he declared.

As for Christian unity, looking back on the age of faith, hope and conflict he said: 'The contentions between the Greek Church and the Roman, the Papists and the Protestants, the Lutherans and the Calvinists, have woefully hindered the Kingdom of Christ.'

Several of Baxter's hymns are still sung today. One was first printed in *The Poor Man's Family Book* in 1672:

Ye saints that toil below
Adore your Heavenly King,
And onward as ye go
Some joyful anthem sing.
Take what he gives – and praise him still,
For good or ill who ever lives.

Richard Baxter's long earthly life came to an end in 1691. He had been a faithful witness through a century of intellectual and physical struggle. The future would bring new challenges.

TEN

ENLIGHTENMENT AND AWAKENING

THE 18th century is often called 'The Age of Enlightenment'. This does not mean people were wiser, kinder or more saintly than those who lived in 'The Dark Ages' but that many were better informed about the world and how it worked.

The word 'enlightenment' translates the German word *Aufklärung*, which literally means 'clearing up'. Enlightenment thinkers believed that new understanding had swept away the clouds of superstition, ignorance and intolerance that had afflicted former ages. Many turned away with disgust from the religious wars of the previous century. The poet Samuel Butler (1612-1680) wrote with contempt:

> *Such as do build their faith upon*
> *The holy text of pike and gun;*
> *As if religion were intended*
> *For nothing else but to be mended.*

The Rise of Natural Philosophy ('Science')
During the battle of Edgehill, which disturbed Richard Baxter's sermon, King Charles entrusted his young sons to the care of his personal doctor, William Harvey. It is said that Harvey sat under a hedge reading a book during the bitter conflict. But the king's physician was much more than a royal childminder – he was a pioneer in medical progress who discovered the principle of the circulation of the blood through the body.

Harvey was one of the 'natural philosophers' or 'scientists' (though the word 'scientist' was not used until the 19th century) who changed our understanding of the world. Telescopes uncovered the secrets of the stars, and microscopes the mysteries of bacteria. Of crucial importance was the theory of gravity expounded by Sir Isaac Newton (1642-1727), which provided mathematical proof that the earth revolved round the sun, and not the other way round. The poet Alexander Pope declared:

> *Nature and nature's laws lay hid in night.*
> *God said, 'Let Newton be' and all was light.*

Newton's discoveries showed that the universe obeys regular laws like a huge machine. But if so, how can God provide loving care for each soul?

One answer was **Deism.** Deists believed God was like a great clockmaker – he had wound up the world at the beginning of time and left it to run by itself. But this left little room for miracles and answered prayer.

But if the Deists were right there was no need for each country to have an established Church. The revolutionary call for toleration made by Roger Williams in the previous century came to look respectable. Enlightenment thinkers came to agree that only really wicked, harmful ideas should be banned by the state.

But what was wicked? Then as now, people argued about this. Was it harmful, for example, to question the truth of Holy Scripture? In 1678 a Deist, Samuel Reimarus, wrote his *Apology for the Reasonable Worshippers of God.* He argued that the writers of the Bible were fanatics who made up much of the sacred story.

Such ideas were too dangerous to publish at the time. Only in 1774 did the poet and critic G. E. Lessing publish parts of Reimarus's writings. This led to a furious controversy with J. M. Goeze, chief pastor of Hamburg, as well as with J. S. Semler, a pioneer 'liberal theologian' who tried to reconcile the traditional faith with the new insights of biblical criticism.

Goeze thought Lessing was undermining the Christian faith, while Lessing considered Semler's 'updated' Christianity to be even more of a menace than Goeze's old fashioned theology.

Such three-sided arguments between secularists, conservative and liberal Christians would be repeated many times in years to come.

Two revolutions

The ideas of the Enlightenment were to inspire the **American Revolution**. A number of the Founding Fathers of the United States of America were Deists – among them Thomas Jefferson – who in 1777 drafted the Declaration of Independence, stating: 'We hold these truths to be self-evident, that all men are created equal, (and) that they are endowed by their Creator with certain inalienable rights, that among these are life, liberty and the pursuit of happiness.'

In contrast to the ancient kingdoms of Europe, the Founding Fathers insisted on the separation of Church and state. The state could not set up an 'established religion' but neither could it control or interfere with the life and worship of believers. Former US President Jimmy Carter writes: 'Separation of Church and state doesn't just protect religion from government meddling. It is also a positive good, encouraging Americans to support hundreds of varied and active religious denominations.'

The French Revolution

Ideas of the Enlightenment also inspired the **French Revolution** of 1789, but now there was – for the first time in Europe – an all-out attempt to get rid of Christianity. The Cathedral of Notre Dame in Paris was used for the worship of the 'Supreme Being' – the God of Deism. The revolutionary leader Maximilian Robespierre acted as High Priest, wearing a specially made sky-blue coat for the occasion. But already the revolution had turned into a bloodbath. In Paris the Reign of Terror was in full swing. Two days after appearing as High Priest, Robespierre was overthrown and put to death on the guillotine, still wearing the sky-blue coat.

Ideas derived from the Enlightenment could open the door to great evil as well as great good. They certainly gave Christians plenty to think about.

Christians learn from the Enlightenment

Believers had to rethink their understanding of **God's providence**, his way of working in the world. They discovered, for example, that victory on the battlefield did not mean that God gave his blessing to the winning side, as Oliver Cromwell sometimes thought. In western Europe they also came to understand that **witchcraft** was an illusion. Slowly witches came to be regarded as harmless fun figures like fairies or pixies. The last person condemned to death for witchcraft in Europe was in Switzerland in 1792, although in many parts of the world people still believe in the evil reality of witchcraft, and this causes serious 'culture clashes' when ideas meet.

Christians had new questions to face. Did miracles really happen? If so, which ones were true? How could you answer the attacks on the truth of the Bible? Was the world really created in 4004 BC? That was the date worked out by Archbishop James Ussher (1581-1666), based on the best scholarship of the time. But now it appeared that the universe could be much, much older. And what of the natural creation? There were many different kinds of animals in South America (let alone Australia – not yet known to the wider world). How could they all have come out of the ark?

Christians face changing times

In Europe there was the beginning of the Industrial Revolution, following the invention of the steam engine, which provided power for industry. Thousands of people began to leave their villages – and their parish churches – behind them. As they crowded into the new and overcrowded towns the old parish system broke down. Who would bring the new faith to them, and to the countless millions around the world?

New songs for new times

By the beginning of the 18th century, in English-speaking lands, Sternhold and Hopkins' 'Old Version' of the Psalms and Scriptures had been replaced by the 'New Version' composed by Nahum Tate (1652-1715) and Nicholas Brady (1659-1726). Even today, many Christians sing the Tate and Brady version of the Christmas story:

> *While shepherds watched their flocks by night*
> *All seated on the ground,*
> *The angel of the Lord came down,*
> *And glory shone around.*

Next, the poet **Isaac Watts** (1674-1748) went beyond the Calvinist tradition of 'Psalms only' in worship and composed many classic hymns, such as:

> *When I survey the wondrous cross*
> *On which the Prince of Glory died,*
> *My richest gain I count but loss,*
> *And pour contempt on all my pride.*

Hymn writing and singing was to play an important part in the work of the Wesley brothers, leaders in **The Great Awakening**.

The Wesley brothers

John Wesley (1703-91) and his brother **Charles** (1707-88) were born and brought up in the parsonage of Epworth, Lincolnshire. While studying at Oxford University they started the Holy Club – a fellowship of committed young Christians. Because of their methodical practice of prayer and Bible study they were mocked as 'Methodists' but the nickname became a badge of honour.

After a less-than-successful mission to Georgia, in America, the brothers returned to England. While on board ship John Wesley was impressed by the steadfast faith of some other passengers who were Moravian Christians, a group whose traditions went back to the radicals of the Reformation. Back in London, on 24 May 1738, at Aldersgate in London, he experienced a time of spiritual awakening. Famously, he wrote: 'In the evening I went very unwillingly to a society in Aldersgate Street, where one was reading Luther's preface to the Epistle to the Romans. About a quarter to nine, while he was describing the change which God works in the heart through faith in Christ, I felt my heart strangely warmed ... and an assurance was given me that he had taken away my sins, even mine.'

The pioneer Salvationist George Scott Railton thought this was John Wesley's conversion experience, so in his pamphlet, *John Wesley the Saved Clergyman*, he depicted the 'unsaved clergyman in the storm'.

Reaching the People

The Wesley brothers were determined to carry the gospel to all, especially those who did not attend parish churches. As opposition grew, they would preach in the open air wherever people could hear. This was sensational, and often large crowds would gather. John recorded in his journal: 'Yesterday, between 12 and one o'clock, while I was speaking to some quiet people, a drunken rabble came with clubs and staves, in a tumultuous and riotous manner. I had scarcely gone 10 yards when a man struck me with his fist in the face with all his might.'

Converts were formed into Methodist Societies, because John Wesley, himself an Anglican clergyman, did not want to form a new denomination or separate from the Church of England. But he would not be restricted either, saying: 'I look on the whole world as my parish.'

George Whitefield (1714-70), who was also a former member of the Holy Club, was another outstanding preacher in the great revival, on one occasion addressing a crowd of 20,000 people on Kennington Common, near London. And that in a day when there were no microphones!

But Whitefield and Wesley came to disagree upon an important point of theology. Whitefield was a Calvinist who believed in

Top left: Athanasius of Alexandria; **top right:** Patrick, patron saint of Ireland; **above left:** Benedict of Nursia (detail from fresco by Fra Angelico); **right:** Justin the Martyr (Justin of Caesarea).

Top left: Martin Luther; **top right:** Pope Julius II (birth name Giuliano della Rovere); **above left:** Johann Tetzel; **right:** John Calvin (1509 – 1564).

op left: Henry VIII, King of England 1491-1547; **right:** Pope Pius V (birth name Antonio ihislieri); **above left:** Council of Trent; **right:** Ignatius of Loyola, founder of the Society f Jesus (the Jesuits).

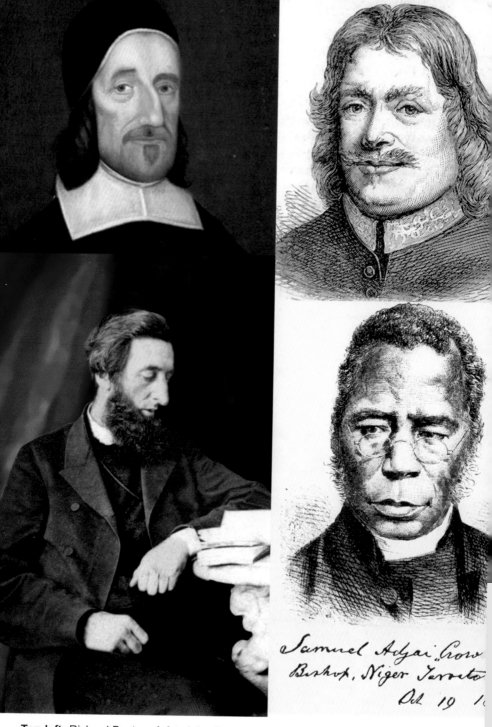

Top left: Richard Baxter; **right:** John Bunyan; **above left:** General William Booth, Founder of The Salvation Army; **right:** Bishop Samuel Adjai Crowther.

predestination – a belief that Christ died only for the elect whom God had chosen. The Wesley brothers followed the opposite teaching of the Dutchman Jacob Arminius (1560-1609), who taught that Christ died for all and that human beings are free to follow him or not. Thus Arminian theology is expressed in many classic Wesley hymns, such as:

For all my Lord was crucified,
For all, for all my Saviour died.

Similar Arminian theology is found in The Salvation Army's articles of faith, which declare: 'We believe that the Lord Jesus Christ has by his suffering and death made an atonement for the whole world so that whosoever will may be saved.'

John Wesley also stressed the doctrine of Perfect Love – the belief that the Christian should strive for a truly sanctified life. Jesus said: 'Be perfect, as your Heavenly Father is perfect' and Charles Wesley expressed this longing in a famous hymn:

Now let thy Spirit bring me in,
And give thy servant to possess
The land of rest from inbred sin,
The land of perfect holiness.

Holiness teaching, understood in different ways, has been important for many Christian believers who belong to the Methodist tradition.

The split with the Anglican Church
John Wesley declared: 'I live and die a member of the Church of England, and no one will ever separate me from it.' But sadly a split became inevitable. Methodist Societies were beginning to look more and more like a separate denomination. Their work depended on unpaid local preachers, laymen and, sometimes, women. And what was to be done in North America?

Across the Atlantic, **Francis Asbury** (1745-1816) was leading the work. But then war broke out between the newly proclaimed United States of America and Great Britain. Who could provide leadership for the Methodists, and how was it to be done?

Within the Anglican Church only bishops could ordain men to the ministry, and the English bishops refused to ordain anyone to undertake Methodist work in America. John Wesley came to believe that he, as a presbyter, had authority to ordain leaders himself, provided they served outside England. So in 1784 he appointed Asbury and Thomas Coke (1747-1814) as 'Superintendents' to lead the American work. Superintendents were soon renamed 'bishops', and American Methodism became independent of the Anglican Church.

The Revivalist Tradition

The young USA was a nation on the move. All through the 19th century the frontier was moving westward and new settlements were established, often beyond the reach of existing church organisations.

One answer was the 'circuit rider', a local preacher who rode on horseback from place to place offering the good news – just as others offered alcohol and guns. His task was to 'revive' the faith among the pioneering people.

Methodist and Baptist Christians were the most successful. In 1783 there were 50 Methodist churches in the USA. By 1820 there were 2,700. Asbury demanded much self-sacrifice from his travelling preachers. Until 1810 he urged them not to marry. Sixty per cent of the Methodist travelling preachers died before they reached the age of 40.

Now efforts were made, not before time, to reach black slaves with the gospel. John Wesley had said that slavery was 'against all the laws of justice, mercy and truth'.

The camp meeting and Salvation Army practice

A popular Christian event at this time was the **Camp Meeting** – an open-air occasion full of enthusiastic prayer, praise and preaching. Several features of this were to influence the future Salvation Army.

The preacher stood on a 'platform' not in a pulpit, and the sermon was often known as the 'Bible address'. Hymns became 'songs'. Below the platform would be the 'Mourner's Bench' or 'Penitent Form' where people seeking forgiveness were invited to kneel. Converts were encouraged to testify straight away to their new and happy experience of God.

By the beginning of the 19th century American revivalist preachers were recrossing the Atlantic to work in the United Kingdom. One – the Methodist James Caughey (1810-91) – was to visit Nottingham in England. There he had great influence on a young man, the future General William Booth.

ELEVEN

LIGHTS IN DARKEST ENGLAND – AND THE WORLD

The story of The Salvation Army

WILLIAM Booth was born in Nottingham, England, in 1829. At the age of 13 he was forced to give up school and was apprenticed to a pawnbroker (a kind of money lender). As a lad he was influenced by speeches made by the social reformer Fergus O'Connor. Many years later, in his book *In Darkest England and the Way Out* William Booth wrote: 'The helpless misery of the poor stockingers [textile workers] of my native town kindled in my heart yearnings to help the poor which have continued to this day.'

But William was not to have a career in radical politics. In 1846 the American revivalist minister James Caughey came to Nottingham. 'He was an extraordinary preacher,' wrote William, 'filling up his sermons with thrilling anecdotes and vivid illustrations.'

The young William Booth and his friends undertook mission work among the poor. 'I saw that success in spiritual work [depends] on the employments of such methods as were dictated by common sense, the Holy Spirit and the Word of God,' said William.

The young William Booth moved to London and went on working for a pawnbroker until a businessman, Edward Rabbits, offered him 20 shillings a week to work for three months as a full-time evangelist. It was in Rabbits's house that William first met Catherine Mumford, who became the love of his life.

Catherine was born at Ashbourne in Derbyshire, also in 1829. As a child she was often ill, so had to spend much time at home, reading and studying. In 1846 she announced that she had found a living faith. In the words of Charles Wesley she declared:

My God, I am thine;
What a comfort divine,
What a blessing to know that my Jesus is mine!

William and Catherine were married in 1855 and William became a minister in the New Connexion, one of the branches of English Methodism. With Catherine at his side, and a young family to support, he still longed to work as a full-time travelling evangelist but his denomination's Conference refused to accept this. So in 1861 William Booth resigned from the Methodist New Connexion.

Meanwhile Catherine was concerned about the subordinate role of women in the Church. When two visiting American preachers, Samuel Palmer and his wife Phoebe, came over to England to conduct revival campaigns, Mrs Palmer had caused a sensation by speaking in public. In her defence, Catherine Booth wrote and published *Female Ministry - or Women's Right to Preach the Gospel.* If the New Testament was rightly understood, she argued, it did not prohibit women from leading and speaking in Christian worship.

As freelance evangelists William and Catherine did not find it easy to support themselves and their young family. In 1865 they returned to London, and later in the year were invited to take part in a mission in the East End – the poorest part of the city. A tent had been erected on a disused Quaker burial ground. Would William accept temporary oversight? He did, and thus The Salvation Army was born.

The East London Christian Revival Mission, set up after the tent mission, grew slowly, but by 1878 it had spread to other parts of the country and was known as The Christian Mission. Its structure was similar to that of the Methodist New Connexion, with an extra item: 'godly women ... shall be employed as preachers'.

Further impetus was provided by the arrival of the fiery and talented George Scott Railton. For 10 years he was to provide new ideas about mission and evangelism. Railton would write to 'General Superintendent' William Booth as 'My dear General', with himself as 'your ever-to-be faithful Lieutenant'.

From Christian Mission to Salvation Army

By 1878 the Mission was on the move. Many new converts were arriving, who cared little for traditional church culture. A pamphlet was prepared which declared 'The Christian Mission is a Volunteer Army'. But Bramwell Booth, William and Catherine's eldest son, pointed out that the 'Volunteers' were part-time soldiers, and he was full-time in the Lord's work. The wording was changed to read: 'The Christian Mission is a Salvation Army.'

In the next four years changes took place which have lasted to the present day. Titles were reversed, and the new movement was renamed 'The Salvation Army, also known as The Christian Mission'. Colourful military terminology, which appealed to many at the time, became part of the set-up. The first yellow, red and blue flag was presented to a local centre by Catherine Booth in 1882. 'Evangelists' became 'captains' and brass bands – the pop music of the day – were used instead of church organs.

Changes: from General Superintendent to General

There were constitutional changes too. Government by committees was thought to be too cumbersome. The Annual Conference voted itself out of existence and General Superintendent William Booth became General Booth, holding power in the mission plus the right to nominate his successor.

Changes: the sacraments

There were also changes in Christian practice. The new Army followed the Quakers in ceasing to observe the two 'Protestant' sacraments of baptism and the Lord's Supper.

Water baptism

The Christian Mission, like other Methodist denominations, practised the baptism of infants. 'I have in some cases,' wrote Bramwell Booth, 'sprinkled as many as 30 in one service. We have a simple ... formula whereby the parents engaged to give the children over to be the servants of God ... [but] this practice ... had no very strong conviction behind it.' As the practice of infant baptism faded away the Army introduced a service of dedication instead.

Holy Communion

In The Christian Mission the Lord's Supper was celebrated monthly, but some missioners had their doubts. Should not every meal celebrate the presence of the Lord? 'Catherine Booth', wrote Bramwell, 'had a horror of anything which might tend to substitute some outward act ... for the fruits of practical holiness.'

In this, Catherine was supported by Railton, who already saw the spreading Salvation Army as a re-creation of 'George Fox and his Salvation Army two hundred years ago'. They were convinced by the case for a spiritual interpretation. The arguments presented by the Quaker Robert Barclay's *Apology* (1678) would be restated in The Salvation Army's *Handbook of Doctrine* (1933 edition).

William Booth initially hesitated. He asked whether the celebration of the Lord's Supper would help or hinder the work of spreading the gospel. Because of widespread drunkenness, the use of alcoholic wine was out of the question, and there were debates about who should or should not preside. Many mission stations were now headed by women, and, as Bramwell Booth wrote, 'The idea of women administering sacraments was at the time almost unthinkable to many good people.'

So, on 2 January 1882, William Booth wrote in *The War Cry*, The Salvation Army's newspaper: 'If the sacraments are not conditions of salvation, and if we are not professing to be a church ... is it not wise for us to postpone any settlement of the question, to leave it for some other day when we shall have more light?

Meanwhile we do not prohibit any of our own people ... from taking the sacraments.' The temporary arrangement was to become permanent.

Church or mission – or both?

William Booth and his followers were keen to make clear they were a mission, not a church. In their day 'church' was understood to mean a traditional, static and even state-supported institution, while a mission involved lively outreach to the unconverted. A church might stand in a well-to-do area, while a mission hall served the poor.

But this distinction could not last, for mission is a mark of the Church. All churches should attempt outreach work, and missions often turn into churches after two or three generations.

As an **Army**, with a **General**, the new movement spread round the world. By 2007 it was at work in 112 countries, sharing the Christian faith in many languages and very different cultures.

Evangelism and social work

From the very beginning, Salvationists were concerned to save souls, for Jesus taught that human beings did not 'live on bread alone' (Matthew 4:4; Luke 4:4). But equally they could not live without it. From his earliest days in Nottingham, William Booth and his friends had undertaken simple charitable help for the poor, and from 1890 – with the publication of his classic book *In Darkest England and the Way Out* – the Army became involved in the widespread social action for which it later became well known.

One victim of the change was George Scott Railton. Like Francis in the Middle Ages, and the 'Non-possessors' in 16th century Russia, he wanted The Salvation Army to remain simple and concentrate on evangelism. In 1894, dressed as a Franciscan Friar, he made a one-man protest against the establishment of The Salvation Army Assurance Society. Many thought the new venture would be a practical way of helping the poor, but Railton was horrified. He publicly tore up the society's application form, and found himself an outsider in the Army to which he had given his life.

Adaptation of measures

Catherine Booth, The Salvation Army's leading thinker, argued powerfully that Jesus had never prescribed any form of organisation to his followers. They were free to adapt their practices to the needs of the time. But The Salvation Army would have to adapt its own measures as it spread round the world. Its methods were those of the revivalist tradition but how could you have a revival among non-Christians? What was there to revive?

As the Army spread round the world it was asked to provide educational, medical and social care. Indeed, it found itself pioneering work for neglected groups in many places.

The pioneer Salvationists agreed with George Fox that you did not need to study at a university before you could begin to preach the Good News. BA ('Born again') was more important than BA (Bachelor of Arts). This is true, but ignorance is not a virtue, and The Salvation Army, like other churches, addressed the problem of providing leadership that was both educated and in touch with the wider public.

Particular witness

Groups of Christians sometimes bear a specific witness which is not shared by all Christian believers. The Society of Friends, for example, maintains a 'Peace Testimony' in opposition to all war.

The Salvation Army, born in 19th century England, shared many of the attitudes of the so-called nonconformist conscience. These included – and for very good reason – opposition to alcoholic drink, drug-taking, gambling and 'worldly amusement'. Many nonconformist Christians did not take part in dancing, go to theatres or visit the cinema. These and other customs would need rethinking as the Army developed in very different cultures and faced the challenges and opportunities of radio, television and the internet. One specific witness, however, was written into the salvation soldier's pledge – the promise to abstain from all intoxicating drink.

Cult of personality

William Booth had been an autocratic General with the power to name his successor – a right he exercised by nominating his eldest son Bramwell. By 1929 the Booth family had become very prominent in Salvation Army life and it was feared the elderly Bramwell would in turn appoint another Booth to succeed him. In that year, therefore, an emergency clause was invoked and a High Council of senior officers was called, which decided that Bramwell's ill health necessitated his deposition. The Salvation Army's constitution was subsequently revised and the election of the General taken over by a High Council of senior officers. Bramwell's successor, the Army's first elected General, was Edward J. Higgins.

TWELVE

SAINTS AROUND THE WORLD

IN the 19th century, as the Church spread round the world it faced many new challenges. For the so-called 'Dark Ages' we are short of good information. St Patrick is one of the few who left a written story. But now many of the great 'cloud of witnesses' are known by name. Here are the stories of three of them. Perhaps they are typical of many others.

Samuel Ajai Crowther – the boy who came back

The Christian faith spread to Africa via Egypt and the Nile, but African churches became isolated by the spread of Islam. In later centuries the Roman Catholic missionaries of the Counter-Reformation attempted work in Angola and Mozambique, but sadly it came to nothing.

In Angola, for a time, there was real progress. King Alfonso – ruler of the Kongo kingdom – was a sincere Christian. In 1526 he wrote to the King of Portugal, asking for medical missionaries. He also added, with emphasis, 'There should not be any trade in slaves or outlet for them.'

His plea failed. As the Atlantic slave trade got out of hand, Christian faith withered. Only in the 19th century did the gospel make real headway. Famous in its story was the future Bishop Samuel Ajai Crowther (1827-1892).

Ajai was born in Oshogun in West Africa (now part of Nigeria). His people worshipped the ancient gods of the Yoruba people – Shango the god of thunder and Ogun the god of iron. The abominable slave trade had long been devouring Africa and when Ajai was still a little lad raiders came to attack his town. His father took his gun and went to defend the stockade that surrounded the town. Ajai never saw him again. His own small bow and arrow were useless. Soon he was taken captive along with his mother. He knew he was a slave and prayed that whatever happened he would not be handed over to the white men. But slaves could be sold and re-sold many times. Soon Ajai was separated from his mother and attached with other men and boys to a cruel chain 40 feet long. It was impossible to sleep at night.

Eventually he was taken to the coast, to the city of Lagos, where he was sold to a slave captain and taken on board a Portuguese ship to sail for America. As they walked down to the lagoon the captives sang 'Pilgrims of earth, come and see us, the pilgrims of Heaven'. The 'pilgrims of earth' were those who were to stay behind. 'The pilgrims of Heaven' were to be sold to the white men and, as they thought, killed and eaten. The Portuguese ship was called *Bona Esperanza* ('The Good Hope'). But Ajai's fortunes were to change. Outside the harbour a ship of the British navy was waiting. The slave ship was captured. Not before time, Britain had turned against the slave trade.

Ajai and his fellow slaves were set free. He was amazed at the sight of the sailors in their baggy trousers and thought the cannonballs on the ship's deck must be human heads. Instead of going to America, Ajai was taken along the African coast to Freetown in Sierra Leone. Here he was cared for by the (Anglican) Church Missionary Society and offered the wonderful opportunity to learn reading and writing. He borrowed a half-penny, ran to the market and bought a card with the letters of the alphabet.

Ajai was introduced to the Bible, became a Christian and was baptised under the name of Samuel Ajai Crowther. After studying in London, Samuel took part in the ill-fated Niger Expedition of 1841. The course of the River Niger had recently been discovered and the plan was for a paddle steamship to sail upriver. The pioneers would set up a mission station in the interior. Thus the new discovery of steam power would help bring the gospel – and honest commerce – to the people.

What looked like a good idea turned into a disaster. No one knew that deadly malaria was caused by a mosquito bite. Non-Africans had no immunity to the disease and died in large numbers. As the steamer retreated downriver Crowther had to help keep the engines running.

It was decided to send a new expedition, this time headed by Africans. Crowther sailed for the west coast again, with a printing press on board. On the voyage he began to translate the Bible into the Yoruba language. Where should he start? He chose to begin with the words: 'Behold, I bring you good tidings of great joy, which shall be to all people' (Luke 2:10, *King James Version*).

During the Yoruba civil wars which had led to Samuel's enslavement, refugees had gathered beneath a great rock known as Olumo. There they had founded a new town, called Abeokuta ('Under the Rock'). Samuel made his way to meet them, accompanied by his young wife, also a former slave. At Abeokuta Samuel told the local chiefs: 'You see here people who were sold as slaves and have come back like men from the dead. This is by the power of God.'

The missionaries were given permission to build a church. Then, amazingly, Samuel heard that his mother was still alive and living a few miles away. Soon they met and embraced each other. Samuel gave thanks to the Lord Jesus Christ for his safe return but his mother praised the power of his dead father's spirit. She did not become a Christian at once but later came to accept the faith and was given the name Hannah (the mother of Samuel in the Old Testament).

In 1857 Samuel Ajai Crowther was made head of the all-African Niger Mission, and in 1864 he became a bishop – the first African bishop since Augustine, 14 centuries earlier.

The rest of the story is not so happy. There were weaknesses in the mission and its churches. Because Crowther had been educated abroad and was not familiar with many African languages some saw him as a 'black Englishman'. Perhaps the work needed outside help on the administrative side but, sadly, it was also undermined by zealous and sometimes intolerant white English missionaries who felt that Christian standards were not being maintained. When Crowther died in 1892 the all-African Niger Mission lay in ruins. Nevertheless some seed had been sown on good ground, especially around the delta of the River Niger.

Josephine Butler: champion of the women's cause

For much of its history the Christian Church has been dominated by men. The New Testament teaches that in Christ there is neither male nor female but it also seems to say that women should keep silent in church. However, the gospel raised the status of women in many parts of the world when it was realised that all are equal in Christ and will certainly be equal in Heaven.

Catherine Booth, the author of *Female Ministry*, was one of the many 'pioneers of the spirit' who pleaded the women's cause in the 19th century. Another was Josephine Butler (1828-1906) who grew up in a prosperous and happy family in the north of England. She was a thoughtful and sensitive child and when her father told her about the wickedness of the slave trade she was horrified. She wrote: 'I saw as in a vision the iniquities practised by men on men, by men on women.'

When she was 17 Josephine went riding in a wood. Suddenly her horse stopped and shuddered before a dark shape hanging from a tree. A local man, a servant, had been sacked by his master and had hanged himself. The shock threw Josephine into spiritual darkness. It took her a year to fight her way back to a deeper faith in God.

Josephine found that women were expected to be seen and not heard. Particularly there were double standards in sexual matters. She wrote to a young man in America: 'The great idea that we combat is the result of the egotism of men and of the deeply rooted idea that the sin of impurity is a greater sin in a woman than in a man. This unequal standard is the devil's invention.'

Nevertheless, Josephine Butler was not hostile to men. She was happily married to the sympathetic George Butler, who helped her begin her public work. He in turn would be mocked and criticised for not 'keeping his wife under control'.

Josephine was upset by a newspaper story telling how a young girl, deserted by her lover, lay in London's Newgate Prison for killing her baby. George suggested, 'Why not write to the prison chaplain and take the girl in as a servant?' Josephine did so. Her life work had started.

She visited the women's prison in the city of Liverpool. 'I was taken to an immense vault filled with women and girls,' she later wrote. 'I sat on the floor and picked oakum' (this meant unravelling old rope, a painful job given to prisoners). 'They laughed at me and told me that my fingers were no use. But we became friends, and I proposed that they should learn a few Bible verses to say to me on my next visit.'

The women prisoners liked Josephine, but others did not. They thought it shocking that a female should undertake public work. 'Women like Mrs Butler', declared *The Daily News*, 'are so discontented in their own homes that they have to be noticed at all costs, and take pleasure in a hobby too nasty to mention.'

The 'nasty hobby' was the fight against unjust laws dealing with prostitution. To cope with the threat of sexually transmitted diseases, 'suspect' women were subjected to compulsory medical examination, while their men clients were exempt. One poor woman wrongly thought to be a prostitute drowned herself in a canal. Josephine Butler launched a campaign to change the law.

In those days, in the United Kingdom, women did not have the vote, but they could still influence the result of elections. During an important by-election in 1870, in Colchester, a mob was out to get Josephine. She took refuge in a hotel but was asked to leave by the landlord after a mob threatened to set fire to the house. Josephine remembered words from Scripture: 'Because thou hast made the Lord, which is my refuge, even the most high, thy habitation; there shall no evil befall thee, neither shall any plague come nigh thy dwelling' (Psalm 91:9, 10 *King James Version*). 'Are they not beautiful words?' she later wrote. 'I felt no more fear and in the strength of these words I went out into the dark street with my friends.'

Josephine also found time to defend The Salvation Army in Switzerland, then under fierce attack. And at a time when Protestants and Roman Catholics were still divided she wrote a life of the Catholic St Catherine of Siena. 'Reader,' she declared, 'if you would understand the visions that she saw, go and live the life of prayer as she did.'

But as Josephine defended the women's cause she knew that 'women's liberation' would bring freedom and dignity to men as well, writing: 'It must be the part of the young manhood of our days to make a place for womanhood. To restore them to their rightful places before the law of God.' Both sexes needed forgiveness, for sexual as for other failings. 'Many a wounded soldier has won the day,' she added, meaning that a young man who had fallen into sexual sin could still be forgiven and go on to treat women with kindness and honour.

Josephine Butler did not foresee the sexual revolution which would sweep the western world in the 20th century. She was not to know about the promotion of pornography and anti-Christian values in the mass media and on the internet. But on the grand issue of relations between men and women she was right: 'The unequal standard was the devil's invention.'

Kagawa – a Japanese man for all seasons

Toyohiko Kagawa was born in 1888. Japan, which had been closed to the outside world for centuries, was changing rapidly but Toyohiko's father followed the old ways and kept a number of concubines, one of whom was Toyohiko's mother. After both his parents died he was left to the care of his father's first wife and his grandmother. They treated him badly. Eventually an uncle sent him to boarding school. There Toyohiko met Dr Myers, a Christian missionary. 'Look at the sky,' said Dr Myers. 'Look at the sun. Let your tears evaporate and you will laugh.'

Toyohiko turned to the Bible and read the words of Jesus: 'Consider the lilies of the field … they toil not, neither do they spin: and yet I say to you, That even Solomon in all his glory was not arrayed like one of these' (Matthew 6:28, 29, *King James Version*). He was a fine poet himself and the words of Jesus enchanted him. He learnt the whole chapter and prayed: 'O God, make me like Christ.' His sadness vanished.

Like Francis of Assisi, Kagawa decided to follow the teaching of Jesus to the letter. Just as Christ lived with the poor of Palestine so Kagawa would live with the poor of Japan. In the Shinkawa district of Kagawa's birthplace, Kobe, people lived in rooms six feet square. He would go and do the same.

His proud family could not accept this 'humiliation'. They drove him out and disinherited him. But Kagawa went further. At one time 10 homeless people were sheltering in his room. He shared his bed with a beggar and developed a serious eye disease as a result.

Was he going too far? How far should Christians go in applying the teaching of their Lord? Jesus told his followers to turn the other cheek (Luke 6:29) if someone struck them, but also advised them to be 'as shrewd as snakes and innocent as doves' (Matthew 10:16).

Poor people were not always grateful, and the pimps and gamblers of Shinkawa suspected that this strange Christian was making money somehow. But Kagawa merely wanted to show love. He gave his shirt to a beggar who returned later and asked for his trousers. Kagawa was reduced to wearing a woman's kimono with a flaming red lining. The joke was all over Shinkawa – what a fool he must be!

But, like Paul, Kagawa was 'a fool for Christ's sake'. His diary in verse, titled *Songs from the Slums*, used the classic beauty of Japanese poetry to share the good news about Christ. He organised 30,000 striking dock workers but preached against violence. He was beaten up and imprisoned for 13 days in jail. While there he wrote a best-selling novel, *The Shooter at the Sun*. 'Only in the Temple of Love do I worship God,' he said. 'In groups of working men, in the bedside of the quarantine hospital where nurses are bravely at work, in the embrace of a loved one, I worship God.'

Sadly Kagawa was to see his country, now on the full flood of industrial development, turn towards war. 'The fault of Japan is the fault of the military party,' he wrote. 'I am not a militarist, nor are the majority of our people.'

The 'military party' did not like that. They liked it even less when Kagawa spoke out in opposition to war against China and apologised to the Chinese for what his countrymen were doing. This, too, he turned into poetry,

For years the Japanese army was victorious, first in China and then against the British, French, Dutch and the USA. But conquest was eventually followed by defeat and the devastation of his beloved country by the atomic bomb.

Kagawa's position became almost impossible. He loved his country and opposed war. Had he betrayed his people? His motives were suspected by both sides but he repeated his promise of 40 years before: 'Throughout the land I go to preach.'

Japanese soldiers returning from their bitter struggles reminded him of the migrating swallows he had watched in his lonely childhood. With words from Scripture in mind he wrote: 'O brothers, coming back empty-handed, desolate, from your sojourn beyond the seas, are you not much better than are these?'

Toyohiko Kagawa died in 1960. The words of the Lord Jesus had guided his long life from start to finish.

THIRTEEN

FAITH, HOPE AND THE FUTURE

The growth of the worldwide Church

AS Richard Baxter looked back on his long life he wondered why Christians had spent so much time arguing and so little spreading the good news to the ends of the earth. Since then much of his hope has been fulfilled, and churches have been planted in many countries where the gospel had been unknown. In this, Bible translation has played a big part.

Some people in those countries have taken a cynical view, declaring: 'Once *you* had the Bible and *we* had the land. Then your missionaries came, and told us to shut our eyes and pray. When we opened them, *we* had the Bible and *you* had the land.'

But the truth is different. Local rulers often had their own mixed reasons for accepting Christian missions. Some wanted their people to 'learn book' rather than hear about Jesus. Then, as now, governments often tried to manipulate the churches for their own political ends.

The end of Christendom

But the century which saw the growth of the worldwide Church also witnessed the decline of 'Christendom' – a society with an entirely Christian outlook, with a single parish church large enough to find room for everybody in the village. Richard Baxter saw the danger when he declined to serve as pastor for the 'free church' set up by Oliver Cromwell's men. Some speak of the end of the Constantinian period, when the Church shared many of the powers of the state.

Now, in most parts of the world, those days are over. 'Christendom' has largely disappeared. Even in lands where there is still a national Church (England, Scotland and the Scandinavian countries for example), the Church no longer has exclusive religious or political power. Indeed the faith has gone into sharp decline in its ancient heartlands of the west. When, in 2005, the European Union attempted to draw up a constitution, references to Christianity were deliberately left out. This has brought gain as well as loss. Ever since the reign of Constantine, Christianity has often been linked with political power. Now, in most parts of the world, the 'Constantinian era' is over.

The rise and fall of Communism
While William Booth was preaching in the East End of London, Karl Marx was hard at work in the British Museum, writing his famous book *Das Kapital* and preparing a new 'gospel'. Marx was an atheist who believed religious belief was 'the opium of the people' – an illusion, persuading the poor to accept their miserable lot. Freedom would come, he thought, through a socialist revolution. His colleague Friedrich Engels made positive, though patronising, references to The Salvation Army, which he said tried to 'fight capitalism in a religious way'. In the 19th and early 20th centuries the new creed of Marxism attracted many eager young intellectuals, much as Calvinism had done in the 17th century.

In 1917, in the chaos of the First World War, the Communists got their chance. Lenin and the Bolshevik party seized power in Russia. The French Revolution had been based on Deism – acting in the name of the 'Supreme Being' – but the Russian revolution put power into the hands of intolerant atheists. The Russian Empire became the Union of Soviet Socialist Republics. Atheism became the 'state religion'. Many churches were demolished and believers were persecuted or killed. In spite of Engels's kind remarks, the Russian Salvation Army was banned in 1923.

Outside Russia many people were deceived by the false gospel of Communism. 'I have seen the future,' said American journalist John Reed, 'and it works.'

In 1949 Communists gained power in China, the most populous country in the world. Here, too, religious believers were persecuted. Missionaries from abroad were expelled. In 1952 The Salvation Army was forced to link up with the 'self-governing, self-supporting and self-propagating state-approved church'. Communism was also imposed on a number of European and Asian countries. All became one-party states, with atheism as the creed of the state.

In Korea, The Salvation Army's Senior-Major Noh Yong Soo was shot by invading Communist troops. As he faced the firing squad, he held up his Bible and declared: 'By believing you can have life.'

But the bright future promised by Marxism turned into a nightmare. Communism was discredited by its failure to provide a better life, and by the brutal cruelty of Stalin in the USSR, Mao Tse Tung in China and Pol Pot in Cambodia. In 1991 the Soviet Union collapsed and the Communist system disappeared from Europe. State atheism lingers in Cuba, and in the People's Republic of China the Communist Party remains in power.

The end of colonialism

In 1900 Britain claimed to rule over 'an empire on which the sun never set'. France and Portugal and The Netherlands also possessed far-flung colonies. But the Second World War was followed by rapid retreat. The independence of India and Pakistan in 1947 was followed by the swift decolonisation of Africa, Indonesia and the Pacific. Large numbers of newly independent countries emerged. Some were successful, while others collapsed into corruption and civil war.

For the churches this meant challenge and change. Many denominations had a colonial structure, with leadership coming from the old imperial countries. British churches tended to have links with former British colonies, German churches with former

German colonies, and so on. The Salvation Army's International Headquarters is still based in London. Some churches have been slow to develop and train local leadership, and even when local leadership emerged, the 'younger churches' often remained financially weak, depending on help from abroad.

Independent churches appeared in a number of countries. Often these provided scope for local leadership when mainstream churches were dominated by missionaries from abroad. Some stressed cultural difference – over polygamy for example. Some sought to combine Christian belief and non-Christian beliefs, but many more were, and are, strongly biblical, stressing healing through faith and opposing witchcraft (whose supporters believe to be a real and evil spiritual force).

The challenge of secular thinking
Very different is the attitude of secular thinkers who, like the Ranters of 17th century England, believe that 'all things come by nature'. Marxism may be largely discredited, but atheist ideas present a strong challenge to Christian faith and thought. You cannot 'save a soul' if the mind is an accidental spin-off of the evolutionary process, for then there is no soul to save.

To present a persuasive answer, capable Christian apologists are needed – thinkers and writers who will do in the modern world what Justin Martyr tried to do in Roman times.

Here it is important to be clear about the meaning of 'secularism'. In the United States, religion is separated from the state precisely *because* it is respected. But other forms of secularism regard religious belief as out of date or an enemy of progress.

The encounter with other faiths
The worldwide spread of the gospel has brought Christians in touch with believers who practise other faiths. In some countries Christians are a minority, coming under pressure from the majority faith which may seek to restrict the spread of the gospel. How

should they respond? It no longer seems right to make crude attacks on the beliefs of others. Everyone has a duty to work together to tackle poverty, disasters and the threat of global warming.

That is why inter-faith dialogue is now in favour. But dialogue must be based on mutual respect and freedom to speak. It must also allow for the possibility of conversion from one faith to another.

How then should Christian believers think of other faiths? Long ago, Christians assumed worshippers of Svantovit – the idol with four faces – were praying to Satan. If not to Satan, to whom? The gospel declares 'Christ is the light of the world' but many people argue that some light is to be found in other faiths as well. If so, how much? Followers of Jesus must not forget his warning that the light in them can also be darkness (Matthew 6:23).

The search for Christian unity

Christian endeavour has spread the gospel around the world and has spread many and various denominations as well. In the 19th century some missions attempted 'zoning' – with Methodists working in one field while Presbyterians planted the faith in another. Such well-meaning arrangements could not last. But concern for Christian unity has led to a great increase in cooperation, notably the establishment of the World Council of Churches in 1948. For the Roman Catholic Church the Second Vatican Council (1962-5) brought great changes in worship and theology, with greater openness to other Christians, and indeed to other faiths.

The Salvation Army was a founder member of the World Council of Churches, but the relationship on The Salvation Army's part was uneasy. In the early 1980s The Salvation Army resigned its full membership and was granted 'fraternal status as a world confessional body'. Its current status is that of a 'Christian World Communion', in which capacity The Salvation Army works together with fellow believers around the world, playing a highly-active part in ecumenical life at local, national and international levels.

'Liberal' and 'conservative' Christians

Disagreements over the World Council of Churches reflect the tensions between 'liberal' and 'conservative' Christian thinking. Is the theory of evolution compatible with faith in a living, loving God? How do believers answer arguments that go back to Reimarus questioning the truth of the Bible? How can the Church adapt its practices to local faith, culture and beliefs? Is today's Church sailing before the wind of the Holy Spirit or drifting aimlessly with the tide of secular thinking? Here are deep questions which have concerned the Church from the beginning.

Justin the Apologist dressed as a Greek philosopher and recognised the thinker Socrates as 'a Christian before Christ'. He went as far as he could in adapting the faith to his own culture. But he refused to burn incense to the Roman gods, and died as 'Justin Martyr'. Today's Christians may be called to take a stand under very different circumstances, running with patience the race that is set before them and looking to Jesus, 'on whom faith depends from start to finish'.

INDEX

99

H

Handel, G. F., 46
Harrison, Thomas, 64
Harvey, William, 67
Hawes, Stephen, 39
Henry VIII, 48
Herod Antipas, 2
High Council, 83
Hobbes, Thomas, 35
Holiness teaching, 73
Hus, Jan, 45

I

Ignatius, 12
In Darkest England and the Way Out,
    77, 81
Inca of Peru, 52
Independents, Independent churches,
    61, 96
Industrial Revolution, 70
Inner Light, 62
Ireland, 64
Islam, 35

J

James, brother of Jesus, 5, 8
James VI and I, 48, 49, 59
Jefferson, Thomas, 69
Jesus, Society of (Jesuits), 53, 54
Jews, 37
'John Wesley, the saved clergyman',
    72
Jonson, Ben, 59
Julius II, 43
Justin Martyr, 14, 27, 98

K

Kagawa, Toyohiko, 81, 90, 92
Knox, John, 48

L

Las Casas, Bartholomew de, 53
Lessing, G. E., 68, 69
Levellers, 61
Lord's Supper and Holy Communion,
    7, 14, 51, 62, 79, 80
Loyola, Ignatius, 54
Luke, 3, 4
Luther, Martin, 44, 45, 46, 47, 49

M

Maxentius, 17, 18
Manichees, 25
Mao Tse Tung, 95
Martin (saint), 33
Marx, Karl, 94
Massachussetts Bay Company, 60
Matthew, Gospel according to, 35
Melville, Andrew, 48
Merovech, 33
Methodism, Methodists, 72, 73, 78, 97
Methodist New Connexion, 77, 78
Middle Ages, 37ff
Monastic movement, 20ff
Montanist movement, 14
Moravian Christians, 71
Moscow, 'The Third Rome', 41
Muggletonians, 62
Muhammad, 35

101